Affirmpress

Yolanda Bogert is a proud mother of two, living in rural Queensland. She's a former bookstore owner with her own incredible life story. This is her first book.

YOLANDA BOGERT

How I met my Son

A story of love that transcends gender

Affirm press

Affirm press

Published by Affirm Press in 2016
28 Thistlethwaite Street, South Melbourne, VIC 3205
www.affirmpress.com.au

Text and copyright © Yolanda Bogert, 2016
All rights reserved. No part of this publication may be reproduced without prior permission of the publisher.
All reasonable effort has been made to attribute copyright and credit. Any new information supplied will be included in subsequent editions.

National Library of Australia Cataloguing-in-Publication entry available for this title at www.nla.gov.au.

Title: How I Met My Son / Yolanda Bogert, author.
ISBN: 9780987233332 (paperback)

Cover design by Christa Moffitt, Christabella Designs
Illustrations by Kai Bogert
Typeset in Garamond Premier Pro 12.25/20 pt by J&M Typesetting
Proudly printed in Australia by Griffin Press

The paper this book is printed on is certified against the Forest Stewardship Council® Standards. Griffin Press holds FSC chain of custody certification SGS-COC-005088. FSC promotes environmentally responsible, socially beneficial and economically viable management of the world's forests.

This book is dedicated to the sproggets of the world: the lost, the amazing and the fearless. If you're having trouble finding your own love, take some of ours to see you through. And to those who went before, whose every fought-for step has made things that much easier for the son I love – he knows that he stands on the shoulders of giants, and we will always be grateful.

*'The sea is dangerous and its storms terrible,
but these obstacles have never been
sufficient reason to remain ashore.'
– Ferdinand Magellan*

CONTENTS

How I met my son		3
1	Slipping on the pelvic floor	8
2	Dragon hunts, moonrocks & eeny-meeny-miny-mo	28
3	Not exactly a parenting savant	43
4	Growing green from red dirt	58
5	'As the twig is bent', or 'Thou shalt not do stuff'	87
6	Peddling Books	117
7	Letters from the Brink	139
8	Transverse	171
9	Going Viral	183
10	Penis shopping and practicalities	216
On we plod		232
Glossary		*240*
Some general Australian umbrellatype resources		*242*

To the reader,

Transgender people don't need more cisgender people (those who identify as the gender they were assigned at birth) speaking for them. What they need is more cisgender people listening to them.

This is our story. We're just a bunch of schmucks from Queensland, and one of us just happens to be transgender. While I've included some general information about transgender issues in this book, I don't speak for anybody but myself (and sometimes Kai, where he's asked me to include something he wanted said). Transgender people are individuals, as different from each other as you are from the person standing next to you. While there may be commonalities, if you want to know something about the transgender person in your life, and if that thing isn't inappropriately intimate, and if that person doesn't mind you treating them as a walking teaching tool, try asking them. Otherwise, the internet is your friend.

Transgender voices are too often shushed and suppressed, or dismissed. I recognise that the privilege I have as a non-transgender person enables me to be heard where they may not be. My hope in taking this opportunity to speak isn't to speak over or for, but to speak alongside, with the sincere wish that it will contribute to visibility that will help to enable their voices in some small way in the future.

Yolanda xoxox

MY SPROGGET CAME into my study and said, 'Have you got a minute, Mum?'

'Sure. What's up?'

He took a deep breath. 'So ... you know how you've always thought that you have a son and a daughter? Well, you actually have two sons.'

'Oh. You're trans?'

'Yeah.'

'Okay. It's cool. Love you.'

'Love you too.'

And we laughed a bit, and I hugged him.

'What? You thought you'd get a different response?'

'Nah. Not really. It's just ... finally out there, yanno?'

'Yeah. Are you keeping your name or do you have another one?'

'Kai.'

'Kai? I like it.'

Then Kai he was. The sky didn't fall and our family didn't fall apart. We just started using different pronouns. Oh, I had to change the name stored in my phone with his number. That was a bit of a pain. Seriously, though, he didn't grow a second head. The earth didn't open up and swallow us for the egregious sin of acknowledging his gender and loving him still.

I could tell he was nervous – but I do hope he already knew that his announcement wouldn't change a single thing about our relationship except for the pronouns we use. Actually, *all* children should know that. In an ideal world, it would be a profound and fundamental truth that they know in their bones. The one unshakeable gravity-fact they carry with them forever. If you haven't actively told yours that you will love and support them, no matter what, and that their sexuality and gender expression are entirely irrelevant to the way you feel about them and treat them, then you need to stop reading this right now and go and tell your sprogs.

Come on. Go tell them now. It's okay, I'll wait. Stare deep into their eyes in that way that makes them really uncomfortable, so they know that you mean it.

It seemed a bit of an anticlimax, really. Kai had had this profound personal epiphany, but no angels flew down to perch on his shoulder and sing the *Hallelujah Chorus*, no cheerleaders jumped out to yell, 'Ra-ra-ra!' There was just us, sitting in my little study and accepting it with a shrug and a hug. It felt like it should be more of an occasion. Our folk don't really stand much on ceremony, but we do know how to celebrate the things that matter, and our kids are definitely things that matter.

I read somewhere that children are more likely to believe positive messages from their parents when they're delivered indirectly. Tell them to their face that you think they're clever or beautiful, and they'll roll their eyes because you're their mum. You have to say that. But let them overhear you telling someone else that you're proud of them and that they have qualities you cherish, and it somehow breaks past that little gate in their brain that assumes maternal bias and settles into their self-image.

So I told everybody. Inadvertently, for the most part. I put a light-hearted retraction in the birth notices section in the back corner of a local paper, thinking that it would make Kai smile – he'd be able to clip it out and have it as a keepsake. But someone else thought it was sweet and shared it on Twitter. The next thing I knew, millions of people around the world had seen it too.

Kai

Why is this such a big deal? I'm just not that interesting. I don't really understand why people went nuts at the birth announcement in the paper, or why people want to read about my life now. Parents sign up for the whole package – I think maybe somebody should put it in the parenting manual that they don't get to decide what that package is, because it seems like it's a surprise to too many people. Childhood isn't the part where you get to create a person: it's the part where you get to know a whole person who already happened.

If you're reading this book because your kid just came out as trans and you want to figure out who they are and what's going on for them, then maybe you should put it down and go talk to them instead. I'm not them.

Coming out was probably the most important thing I could have done for myself. Holding on to the secret almost hurt. But while it was the best thing, it was also the most frightening.

It's certainly not a thing to be taken lightly, and as a professional procrastinator I put it off for a long time. I desperately wanted to openly be myself. Even though I wasn't exactly certain who that was, I knew that the person who I was presenting wasn't entirely me.

Coming out at school would have involved a whole sack of problems. I was already perceived as an oddball lesbo dyke and wore all of the bull that goes with it, so adding transgender to that pile would probably have been more than I could take. Though I had a small circle of supportive and accepting friends, most of them dealing with their own sexuality and gender identity issues, high school was a pretty lonely place for me.

After graduation, the night that decided me involved, as many significant life events do, alcohol, a trampoline and stargazing. In a moment of whimsical conversation, I asked a close friend how she would react if, hypothetically, I told her that I was transgender. It was the first time that I'd verbalised it, and suddenly, as if I'd breathed life into it, it became real to me. My friend paused before she answered me, probably just a second at most, but it felt like a bajillion years. She said that it wouldn't bother her, that I would still be me, and I got my first taste of acceptance.

Once I'd made the decision to tell Mum, I felt like I had the same kind of nerves I got before giving a talk in front of my class. Mega anxiety with shaky hands and my heart pounding in my ears. Though, unlike with a lot of teachers, I knew that my mother would still love me no matter what came out. But even though I knew for a fact that she wouldn't do anything other than love me unconditionally, there was still fear. Irrational fear, but fear nonetheless. I guess that's why they call it irrational.

So I took a deep breath, and told her who I was.

1

Slipping on the pelvic floor

I FEEL A BIT of a squick reading the comments of a hundred thousand people telling me that I'm a great mum, given that I've never considered myself to be especially maternal. I've been a mother my entire adult life and some of my childhood too, but I never actually thought that I was any good at it.

How on earth do other parents manage to keep pairs of socks together and have the same lunchboxes for the *entire* year – with the right lids, no less! How do you consistently have spare clean towels folded neatly in the airing cupboard so that they're ready to use, without having to leave wet footprints all over the house looking for a handtowel or a dry facewasher – a goddamn paper towel or a tissue, even – or anything to dry yourself with because the sprogs have run off with every last one?

And what's with the *bits*? The icky crumbs of seemingly nothing recognisable that find their way under sofa cushions and work their way between car seat grooves, and multiply like Tribbles wherever kids have been. What is that stuff, and why don't other people seem to have it?

~

I had a beginning in 'interesting times' – the kind from the old curse, not the good kind.

I was fifteen when I fell pregnant with Kai, and I had him just a couple of months after my sixteenth birthday. You might be making some assumptions, some of which might even be true. Some are less true, but I might even agree with you on them anyways.

It's easy to internalise the shitty labels that teen pregnancy slaps on you, particularly when you haven't yet grown enough to wallpaper yourself with your own labels. This manifested in all sorts of odd ways, not least of which was an overwhelming sense that while other parents were actually parenting, I was just playing at it. That my nurturing was practice – an imitation.

I've often joked that I'm surprised my sproggets have survived my parenting attempts thus far, but whenever I've said that, there's always been a little voice in my head meanly claiming the underlying truth of it. I know the infant mortality rates and statistical disadvantages for children born to teen parents. Just as I know that there's much more to being a parent than reminding the kids to tuck a hanky in their sleeve, or telling them that their current love interest isn't good enough for them, or disparaging their housekeeping style.

Me getting pregnant is a story as old as ... a really old thing. Throw a traumatised teenage book nerd, who has low self-esteem and few expectations, together with an older Neanderthal boyfriend, and she can romanticise his stoicism and interpret his intentions as whatever she likes. 'Meh. You want a Coke?' definitely translates to that teenager as 'Yes, I'm just like Heathcliff and you're so Cathy.' Mix in a secretive sorta-kinda education in sexual health, dictated by conservative policymakers and awkward parents, and you end up with a shiny new bun in a fifteen-year-old oven. We could examine socioeconomic and psychosocial contributing factors too, but who wants to trudge through that yawnfest just for a thorough story?

The best place to start anything is at the beginning. I don't mean the beginning of Kai – nobody needs those details – but the beginning of me feeling this way about him. The very first seed of it was planted while fifteen-year-old me sat across the desk from a doctor in Newcastle's anonymous sexual health clinic. He looked sad as he showed me my pregnancy test and told me what it meant.

Right there. That sad look on his face, that he must have worn fifty times a week when he told other fifteen-year-olds that they were pregnant. I already understood the hopelessness he was trying so hard to be too professional to convey, and I could see a whole lot more of it coming when every other person I knew found out. I could almost feel their collective sigh.

I felt terrible that a deep little corner in the back of my mind was wearing such a grin as you never saw.

There's no way to get across just how naughty it felt, to be carrying this small secret joy around – for it was quite some time before I could share it with anybody. It wouldn't have been proper. I was fifteen and pregnant, the sky was falling, and I'd broken the world irreparably forever. Apparently. The only proper response to express when you've done that is chagrin and shame and mourning for the brilliant and shiny hypothetical life that my recklessness had cost me.

Though I hadn't even met Kai, I already loved the idea of him. He wasn't some growing doom that would soon come crashing down on my head. He was everything that was precious and pure. He was the brilliantly white lacy baby socks that I packed in a plastic bag inside a box so that the general ick of life couldn't taint them before he came to wear them. He was the (figurative) embodiment of all the things that I hadn't even thought to dream of, because I didn't know that I was allowed to have them. A person in the world for whom I wasn't a burden, or work, but a source of the good stuff.

Sure, it was scary. Not so long before this, I'd forgotten that I'd taken my pet mouse out to play and accidentally smushed her. What could I possibly offer Kai other than a lifetime of neglect and poverty? I, who couldn't even remember a mouse? There was no shortage of folk around to remind me of this particular angle of thought.

I can't help but feel a little robbed of some of the shared joy that I should have had then. When I told people about the very first time I felt him move inside me, like little butterfly wings (or like the bubbles after you fart in the bath), their response was mostly bittersweet – that it was a lovely thing, but beneath those words was still the unspoken wish that I'd do the sensible thing and have an abortion. Life certainly would have been much simpler that way. But it wasn't right for me then, and there was no turning back time, so I was going to love him so hard that his head popped off. I didn't have anything else to offer him at all, so it was just going to have to be enough.

Still, even all these years later, I feel like I should be ashamed of being pregnant then, but I just can't bring myself to.

~

We already had baby all over the place, because my sister, Shelley, gave birth to Kai's cousin, Josh, three and a half months before he was born. It had been strange to bring a baby into a family that hadn't seen one for more than a decade. There was resistance at first – it took a while for precious things to be tucked away and temporary allowances made for the less-mobile and height-challenged.

Josh was a simply enormous ten-pound baby that Shelley had hidden away in a teeny-tiny bump. So, of course, being the tactful and considerate folk that our people can be, everybody would eye off my massive belly knowingly and tell me that I must be carrying the

Incredible Hulk Baby. Surely telling me of the dire things to expect would alleviate the apprehensions and fears that I had about labour, right? Right.

Mine was a particularly uneventful baby-carrying, aside from some low blood pressure and insane cravings that induced a violent need for cheesecake. Then again, I like cheesecake just as much when I'm not feeding a parasitic invader, so I suspect that may just be hokum I made up.

Kai's due date was in the middle of July, but given that his birthday is in August, he obviously didn't show up on time. Fourteen days overdue. Anyone who has been pregnant can tell you that it felt like fourteen weeks. None of the concerns of teen parenthood applied anymore. It didn't matter how I was planning on supporting a baby without a job or an education. Because I was going to be pregnant FOREVER, and he was NEVER coming out.

He did, though. Like all babies, in his own good time. Very quietly one evening, just before bedtime, I got some niggly cramps and I knew he was on his way. So I said goodbye to Grandma, told her that his name was going to be Elizabeth Anne, but we'd call him Beth, and Aunty Shelley drove me to the hospital. (*Aunty Shelley driving was way scarier than my impending labour, Kai ... but you know that, you've seen her behind the wheel.*)

I'm not going to go into great and gory detail about his birth – he's heard me tell it before, and it's pretty much the same as six and a half billion stories just like it. Suffice to say, it was scary, painful and icky ... but I'd do it a dozen times over if I got Kai at the end of it. I don't think I've ever told him that part.

He was lifted onto my belly, a teeny mewling ball of arms and legs covered in vernix and blood and all kinds of indescribable fluids, and he was the most beautiful yucky little alien I'd ever seen. A dim medical light was spotlighting my bump, and the room quietened reverently as he made his first snuffling sounds. It was surreal. Like opening a gift from a really thoughtful person who got you something that you didn't know you wanted in the first place, but now that it's yours, you don't know what you ever did without it.

He was so impossibly tiny and perfect. I'd swathe him in his swaddling blanket and hold him close. He was always warm, though he weighed next-to-nothing. Sometimes if I let myself look at him long enough, I'd realise that my arms were shaking with the effort it took not to crush him, I wanted to hold him so tightly. It was a physical feeling – still is. When I'm bursting with pride, it's literal. My chest feels like it might puff up so much that it will explode. At the same time, it feels as though someone is squeezing my heart, and I can't breathe properly.

When it was time to take Kai home, I packed up all our things and strapped him into the car capsule to carry him out. I stopped at the front desk to see if there was anything they needed me to sign or do, but the nurse assured me that we'd done everything – goodbye and good luck. I turned to walk out with him and felt sure that someone would stop me. I kept waiting for a hand on my shoulder and a nurse telling me that there'd been a mistake, and they didn't actually let irresponsible and obviously incompetent people like me out into the world with something so utterly precious.

It's hard to describe how I felt, walking to the car, when I realised that I got to keep Kai. Not exactly like I'd stolen him, that doesn't quite fit. But you know that feeling when you come across a treasure in a second-hand shop and see it marked at a fraction of what you'd actually pay for it? Something that you want to hug to your chest and sneak out with, in case the shop owner realises their mistake in letting something so awesome go for such a meagre sum. You set it on the counter tucked between everything else you're buying, and you hope that the owner doesn't notice, then you get out of there quick smart! Yeah, that.

~

There's no doubt that my own teen pregnancy shaped my attitude towards what I taught my sprogs about sexual health. For years, I stocked their bathroom with condoms and made it very clear to them – and encouraged them to make it clear to any other teenage visitors – that they were welcome to them, no questions asked.

I strongly suspect that I was actually just funding a steady stream of water bombs and stick-it-over-your-head party gags, but if just one of those condoms found its way into the hands of some kid who would otherwise have had unprotected sex, then I'm okay with that.

The simple fact is that teenagers who are freely given factual information about sexual behaviours – as well as easy access to practical ways (like condoms and the contraceptive pill) to make responsible choices around sex – have fewer cases of STIs and unintended pregnancies. When kids are already making decisions about sex, why on earth don't some parents give them the unimpeded option of safe decisions?

Kai was much more sensible about that kind of thing than I was at his age. At fifteen, he decided that he wanted the Implanon implant. (Not at my suggestion at all, just in case that's what you're thinking – he makes his own choices.) When he approached me about it, I pretended to consider it sagely, and discussed the pros and cons with him. We googled possible side effects and accounts of other people's experiences with it, so that he was making an informed decision. All the while, I was doing the happy dance on the inside at the thought of him definitively removing himself from potential teen pregnancy statistics and no longer having that as a concern.

So we went to the GP, bought the implant and made an appointment to have it put in. Which is all dandy, except that Kai is terrified of needles and the implant looks like a pointy alien probe. He held his breath and squeezed his eyes shut through the smaller local anaesthetic needle, and that was fine, but then, as soon as he saw the implant, he freaked out and started shaking his head, backing into the corner. No amount of comfort and coddling would convince him that he wouldn't feel it going in.

At this point, now that the sterile packaging had been opened, I was already out a few hundred dollars that I could ill afford for the appointments and the injection itself. I was also reliving the times (time*S* plural) that he had wheedled and begged me to get his ears pierced and then, when the pre-paid earrings were out of the box and he took a look at the needle, he kicked and screamed and didn't want them anymore – until the next time we passed the piercing joint. Bah!

So I growled at him, a bit too harshly, 'There are millions of people the world over who would give their right arm to have this needle, and you're among the privileged few who have access to it. Suck it up, buttercup.'

The doctor and her assistant gave each other a look, and I'm sure they thought that I was a monster, forcing sterilisation on my unwilling kid. Maybe I'm writing this wrong and you think I'm a monster too, but I promise that Kai was fine with the idea of having it. He just needed some ... encouragement for the procedure itself. (I should wave to my mother here – I've got five bucks that says she's laughing her arse off through this story, remembering the time it took two orderlies and a nurse to hold me down for my tetanus shot when I was twelve. Yeah, Mum, go on, laugh it up.)

~

Back in the land of irresponsible teen parents in the 1990s, Kai's father wasn't interested in being one. When I told him that I was pregnant, his response was an eloquent: 'So?'

He hasn't been a part of our story since, by his choice, so that's all the mention he gets. His mother, on the other hand, Kai's nanny, wasn't going to let his indifference stand in between her and her grandbaby. She stormed into our lives with bassinets and strollers, and a giant instant family of uncles and an aunt to adore Kai along with her. It was a huge help – it's an understatement to say that having a baby as a teenager is a bemusing experience.

From when I first found out about Kai's existence, I was fascinated by the whole process of pregnancy, birth and early childhood, and I wanted to learn everything about it. But I was only able to access three levels of information: medical science journals, Average Joe info in the form of *What to Expect When You're Expecting*, and seriously dumbed-down pamphlets that are thoughtfully handed to those of us unfortunate enough to get knocked up at fifteen.

I wasn't assertive or self-possessed enough to articulate this at the time, though, so I'd just say 'thank you' to the medical professional and quietly tuck the *Your Belly Will Get Bigger Now by Dr I.M.A. Patronisingwanker* pamphlet in my folder with the comparative analgesia studies that I'd brought to ask questions about at my appointment. Being seen as a two-dimensional statistic seems the cruellest while you're living a ten-dimensional life in your head.

The medical professionals who cared for us were a bit of a mixed bag. Some of them were just plain lovely, and I know that I got the same smiling care from them that I would have received if I was the vicar's wife having her third. (For that, they have my eternal gratitude.) Others would never say anything outright, but even then I wasn't too stupid to understand exactly why the attending nurse was pursing her lips, or why she tore off her glove and walked out of the room to stop herself from expressing her disapproval. I'm fairly certain the underlying sentiment was: 'Silly little girl. You made your bed, now shut up and lie in it.'

But then, I was swimming with hormones, and life wasn't exactly calm and stress-free, so I may have been projecting some of my insecurities on to them, to be fair. I look back now at the times I felt small, and patronised, and ignorant, and I wonder how much of it was some entitled jackass feeling self-important, and how much was me being self-deprecating. (It has always bothered me that I can't articulate what I want to articulate when I'm feeling that way as a patient. My words seem clumsy and broken, and my frustration at not being able to say what I mean just compounds it. Mostly I close in meekly on myself and bottle it up, then stew about it later. I've become very good at writing letters after the fact – okay, so I mostly don't send them, but they make me feel better.)

Some ignorant young parents really do need 'then the baby comes out of the vagina' type information, but I've often wondered how much the teen-parent stereotype and its accompanying educational, health, developmental and employment statistical outcomes are self-fulfilling. Someone wearing a label of dependency on government benefits is imbued with all sorts of presumed characteristics that make them less employable and increase their dependency on government benefits, for example. Or, the shame and stigma put on teen mothers with the expectation that they won't meet their child's health-care needs increases the likelihood that they will avoid/delay attending health-care services, which results in worse health outcomes for their child. Try getting off that merry-go-round, and the carousel horses come to life and wrap their fibreglass hooves tight around you.

I tended to swing between extreme reactions to that stigma. At times I was so determined not to wear the stereotype that I would be up until 2am, neurotically cleaning the walls with sugar soap and despairing if anything was out of place, or if any part of our home didn't look like some absurd parody of some shiny movie family, which is where I got most of my ideas about what a family 'should' look like. At other times I would vehemently reject judgement and eschew anything remotely respectable as a way to disown the feeling.

What I understood even less was how I'd already created my identity: mother, breeder, domestic. Every one of my achievements and flaws was seen through a 'teen parent' lens that could diminish or magnify, depending on who was looking and what they were looking at.

On one hand, I could rest easy, having fulfilled my proper role as the owner of a uterus and contributed to the gross national product. I would never have to face the bewildered questioning of people with rigid gender role expectations who wondered when, not if, I planned on spawning. (Phew.)

On the other hand, I was now a consumer of resources. Part of the amalgamated Great Unwashed, because there was now a societal obligation to provide for Kai's healthcare, education and safety, without me having already done my share. I was guilty, as the other half of that parental equation would never be, of thoughtlessly procreating. I get to do time for that particular crime every time someone looks at Kai and puzzles over my apparent age. Sometimes I smile and give them a moment to count on their fingers, and other times I rush on to the next part of the conversation so that their thought doesn't have time to form properly and neither do all the preconceptions that go with it.

It wasn't long before I learned that women are also made to feel plenty lesser for not having children. Wasn't too long after that before I figured out that women are just made to feel lesser, full stop. Doesn't matter if you breed or not. Do it young, or old, or in between. Whichever way you do it, it'll be wrong.

~

If I had my time over, it'd be nice to think about planning children properly, if at all. Would I even have had children if I'd waited long enough for the option of not having them to occur to me? And trying it with stability and pre-made financial security would be different, though there are bonuses to having a young parent who hasn't yet had their imaginative soul sucked out by a corporate and commercial world. I felt closer to Kai and Myk'l (a.k.a. Mikey, Kai's little brother, who was born 1998) when we played than I ever did to the adultish side of things, and it seemed like other people were walking around entirely blind to the stuff that we three saw.

More than once, disapproving frowns from strangers in parks were met with a pantomime of exaggerated dysfunction for the pure joy of being antagonistic. I'd light a smoke, scratch my tit and screech out, in an accent dripping with bogan, 'Jim-Bob! Lurlene! C'mon now. We got to get back so Mama can watch her stories!' Everyone takes their amusement where they can get it, I guess, and joys like this are bittersweet when you know that it's art imitating life.

With the disruptions of my early teenage years, then falling pregnant with Kai – Falling? *Wheee!* That needs a better word – my formal schooling was haphazard and short-lived. I think that Year Eight was the last entire year that I finished in an actual school, while Year Nine was completed via distance education. After Kai was born, his grandma, his nanny and his Aunty Shelley took turns looking after him while I did a Year Ten equivalency through TAFE, but it was never really the same.

When I'd been a couple of months along with Kai, I had enrolled myself in the Year Ten class at the school around the corner from my little bedsit. They wouldn't let me sign myself in, given that I was only fifteen and none of their policies seemed to know what to do with that, so my boyfriend at the time played guardian (he was twenty-four and obviously all growed up and mature).

Less than a week went by before I was called in to the year advisor's office and asked if I was pregnant. Then I was asked if I could think of any options for my education other than attending their school. Maybe I should do the best thing for the baby, concentrate on being fecund for the moment and catch up later on? Wouldn't that be better? They didn't want me being jostled in the hallway and coming to harm. They didn't want the other girls seeing it and getting ideas. It was for the best.

The advisor did everything she could to wedge me into the too-hard basket, and she couldn't get me out the door fast enough so that I could 'have a think'. (Gawd, I hate that phrase. It usually just means, 'Go away until you come to the same conclusion that I have, because I'm too gutless to say what I mean outright.' Bah.)

Because I didn't finish high school in the usual way, I've always felt like I missed out. Like the rest of the world is in on some secret that I haven't been told. Like I'm often trying to interpret the obscure pop culture of a whole other generation – on a whole other planet. Formals and graduations and the regular rites of academic passage seem like plot happenings in stories to me, and not actual experiences that real people have, because I can't relate.

I've spent a lot of time in self-education, trying to catch up. I'm a fast reader and, when I've got the time, I can get through a few books a week. That still wasn't cutting it, until I discovered a network of people who think that knowledge is brilliant and should be shared freely, and that no one should be embarrassed because they want to talk about things that matter instead of football and beer. Okay, that was a lie, they totally talk about football and beer, they just talk about it in between the science and politics. It's wonderful when you grow up enough to realise that you can choose friends who value what you value, rather than making a lazy selection because of geographic convenience.

~

Do you remember pushing off on the swings as a child?

You take the run up and get those treated-pine woodchips all through your shoes, so you shake your feet to get them out, and if you're lucky your shoes don't fling off. You do a few casual swings at first, because you're too cool to commit to enthusiastic swinging straight away. You lean right back with your eyes closed until you lose the sense of where your body is in space and realise that you're so far back, your ponytail is dragging on the ground and there are woodchips in your hair. Damn it.

Then you start the serious business of momentum gathering. You push yourself higher. And higher. And higher! You watch the corners of the frame carefully, because with every squeak of the swing, the painted steel shifts just a tad on the bolts holding it down. You can feel it through the chains that your hands are squeezed around, so tightly that it makes your knuckles white and the rust comes off on your skin. You cross your fingers and pray that the bolts aren't rusted all the way through and that they'll break on the next kid's turn, not yours.

You get to that really high point and you wonder if, just maybe, you can go over the top. Until, right at the peak of your arc, the chains slacken and, for a slow-motion moment, nothing is holding you up anymore and it's almost as though you can fly. Close your eyes. You're a bird!

And then you jerk back into the seat and grasp at the chains again, clinging desperately as your heart leaps into your throat and your stomach lands in your shoes, if you're still wearing them, and the swing catches you and goes down.

You feel as though you've touched something magical. The almost-possibility of going over the top leaves you with a sense of the surreal and sacred. The next kid in line knows it too, and they want the nirvana that they've just seen you brush up against.

Back on the ground after I reached those heights, my inner chicken would kick in. I wouldn't be able to get up there again. I'd occupy myself with leaning over the seat and twisting the swing around in circles until the chains were braided up and my feet couldn't touch the ground. Then I'd let go, my eyes closed, and twirl until the chains snapped back the other way and arrested the momentum.

My family grew, and soon Kai would do it on the swing next to me, then later Mikey would do it on the swing next to him – the three of us trying to outspin one another. Magic is inherited.

To my darling former tenant,

We both know that finishing the things that I start isn't one of my special gifts, but writing all this down for you to read has been in my head since I first knew you existed, so I've managed to finish this book.

I know you sometimes feel like you're a burden, or maybe you've felt that I've thought this about you, which is a mistake. You never were. Quite the opposite.

I can't tell you what it was, to have someone ask me questions as though I might know the answers — to look at me like I'm the one to mend the things that are broken and set the world to rights. To be the sage bringer of stories and the haver of judicious instruction. To matter that much for someone. I don't know if I had to be a whole new person for you, or if I already was, but unrealised. Either way, it was great. Having you is great.

I want to write something profound and beautiful here, so that you'll never doubt that you're cherished and loved ever again, but usually when I try to write stuff like that, I just end up sounding profoundly awkward. So many years of floofy internet memes mean that it's hard to express sentiments like love without it sounding clumsy and contrived. I know that doubt and loneliness and sadness aren't especially rational, so I know that you'll still have them the same as everybody else. But when you do, hopefully all you'll need to do is pick up this book to send them away.

Then again, this book could just be one mother's desperate extended campaign to finally get her kid to tidy their room. Seriously, dude, I'm taking out a billboard next.

I have no idea what's coming up for us or whether we'll be able to deal with it, but whatever it is, I think I should face it in pigtails and you should wear your pineapple shirt.
Lots of love,
Your Favourite Oppressor xoxox

2

Dragon hunts, moonrocks & eeny-meeny-miny-mo

I WISH THAT I could introduce you to Kai as a toddler. He stayed relatively tiny as he grew, such a dainty little thing. Every movement made was precise and considered, even as he tore around the world, throwing open doors and windows of discovery on his way. He was so precocious that people found it unnerving when they first met him. It gave me no end of amusement to watch people stoop down to regard him with some condescending sentiment, as they do to small children, only to be met with a perfectly lucid and articulate response.

We'd often take the hours-long train trip to Nanny's house, and there's nothing much to do with an active child on a train except talk and question and teach. Left to his own devices, Kai would want to question everybody in the carriage about the smallest details of their lives and ask them all to share in his sandwich (or ask if he could have a bite of theirs). He was not remotely inhibited, so I had to be pretty vigilant.

One trip, during rush hour, a tidily dressed man shared our seats and struck up a conversation with Kai. The man was a little awkward, as though he wasn't used to children, but politely tried to engage my son. Talk came around to flowers that we could see through the train window, and the man was very pleased to be able to tell all about how the flowers used the sun to make their food.

Kai put his little hands on his tiny hips (he was four years old) and gave that man a look of utter disdain and eternal patience with the silly growed-up. 'No, silly, they use photosynthesis.' His pronunciation was adorable and way off the mark, but it was clear which word he was trying to say.

The look on the man's face was a picture, and I'll never forget it. He looked at me, stunned and gaping like a codfish, and I just shrugged as though Kai did that kind of thing all the time and more fool him for underestimating him.

Kai gets underestimated way too much. We need to stop doing that. When Mikey came along to grow our family by one, we went from partners in awesomeness to colleagues in an expedition team. At least, until the novelty of having a little brother wore off.

~

Mum: What time are you coming home?

                Kai: I'm already home. I did say Hi.

Mum: Oh. I didn't hear you come in.

                Kai: Yes you did, Mum. You said Hi back.

Mum: I don't think I did. I feel like I would remember.

                Kai: Then you brought me my washing and stood talking to me for five minutes.

Mum: Are you sure?

                Kai: Pretty sure.

~

One of the hardest parts about writing this book is having to reflect on things that I don't really want to examine too deeply, in that examining the memory might damage it somehow. Memories are funny like that. I read somewhere that when you remember something, your brain isn't actually thinking back to what happened, it's just replaying the last time that you remembered it, which is why details grow fuzzier. It's like a fucked-up game of cerebral telephone whispers.

I remember sneaking halfway down the stairs one night as a child and sitting there in the dark, watching *The Day of the Triffids* over Mum's shoulder. I remember it as absolutely terrifying. Doubly so because I had to stay quiet or Mum would know that I was out of bed. And in the film, there was something very frightening about not only being overtaken by sentient plants, but even the seemingly omnipotent growed-ups being made vulnerable and blind.

I've had a copy of the original John Wyndham novel on my shelf for ten years, and I've avoided reading it because I had this idea of it being so scary. But then, a few months ago, the movie popped up in my feed and I watched it. Seeing the comical rubbery plants shuffling around and realising that they were probably just prop guys shaking covered broomsticks at the camera was a pretty huge letdown. I'll have to make time to read it now.

I've been similarly betrayed by my own memory of *Clash of the Titans* and *The 7th Voyage of Sinbad*. The vibrant and magical scenes with majestic monsters and epic heroes that I remember fall flat now. I was absolutely in love with Bubo the animated clockwork owl and dreamed of having one of my very own, but now he just seems stiff and inanimate. It's hard to reconcile that they're exactly the same things thirty years later – I'm the thing that has changed. What's happened to my perspective?

My grandma, and then my mum, used to sing our 'morning song' knowing full well that the quickest way to wake a reluctant someone up is to be obnoxiously cheerful. They would come into our bedroom, throw open the curtains and sing: *'The sun has got his hat on / Hip hip hip hooray! / The sun has got his hat on / And he's coming out to play!'* Which, of course, became a favourite childhood recollection and yet more ammo in the Mother Arsenal to mess with my own sprogs. (As a secondary benefit, it works to summon horses and cattle in for their morning feed.)

While writing this book, I looked up the rest of the lyrics and so wish that I hadn't. The second verse (that my mum and grandma never sang, and we never knew) includes the revolting line: '*He's been tanning ni**ers out in Timbuktu / Now he's coming back to do the same to you.*'

Suddenly one of my most cherished childhood reminiscences takes on a sinister tarnish. As with remembering John Jarratt play with Big Ted on *Play School* and then seeing him chase girls through the desert with a rifle in *Wolf Creek*, or even hearing Noni Hazlehurst say 'fuck', I'm not sure how much of my childhood is left to innocence at all. Do John and Noni realise that they're not allowed to do this? That they belong to us and our collective memories? Somebody should tell them.

Not everything changes, though. I still cry when the Black Rabbit of Inlé comes for Hazel, and when Optimus Prime breaks.

So it can be hard to dredge up memories, and harder still because the stories in this book, they're not just mine and Kai's. They're our family stories. They belong to our extended family and friends too, so it's really important to me that I tell them right. Even as I write these things and read them back to myself and Kai, and sometimes Mikey, they feel incomplete. It's so very hard to write a whole person in text – it feels like a scattered mosaic. Thousands of words, and I still don't feel like I'm telling our story with any of the important bits.

For all the struggles and bullshit and general rubbish that humans have to wade through to survive, we've had some amazing times together, our little family. Though, as I'm sitting here and laughing to myself, remembering the whacky things we did to keep ourselves entertained, Kai and Mikey occasionally poke their head into my study to read over my shoulder, 'Huh? What dragon hunt? I don't remember that.' I've therefore come to the conclusion that it's a complete waste of time doing anything with sproggets before they're eleven or so. Just pop them into a cupboard until they're useful – save yourself the trouble.

~

During our single-mother Era of Pecuniary Fuckedupedness, which you might remember better as the Howard administration, I learned some lessons. Like that poverty isn't having to unbolt the back seat of your car to get at the change underneath it so that you can buy bread – no, poverty is remembering that there's change underneath your back seat, but being unable to unbolt it because the damn car was repossessed the week before. Also, that whenever you think you're as broke as you can possibly be, there are inevitably another nine rings of hell lower than where you thought the bottom was.

Even as I type, I'm aware that this is privileged white-person-in-a-prosperous-country poverty. Homelessness when you have a car to sleep in and clothes to change into, while shitty, is still nicer than plenty of other types of homelessness.

There are ways around poverty in Australia, when you're looking for fun. An $0.80 bag of flour makes for at least two days' worth of playdough – and three weeks' worth of picking it out of your carpet.

It only takes six plastic buckets and three trips to the beach to get enough sand to turn a paddling pool into a sandpit. You can fit one and a half little brothers into a front-loading washing machine, but when he breaks the door as he struggles to get out, you'll have to eat two-minute noodles for a fortnight to replace it.

I mastered the art of the hundred-dollar holiday. Two nights in a caravan park at $30 per night, $20 for petrol to get there, $15 for fish'n'chips and $5 for ice-cream. Zero dollars for sitting by the lake while fishing with hand reels and stale bread. *Ta-da!* For two pre-schoolers it was the very definition of heaven.

A couple of times I managed to scrounge enough to hire a houseboat for a week. I think that one day I'll be a defendant in a court case somewhere, and my lawyer will use these houseboat holidays as evidence for my insanity plea. Taking two young children on a houseboat alone in the middle of the Myall Lakes system once is weird enough, but doing it in subsequent years just rests the case.

It was brill. We were privateers, escorting a precious cargo of spices and silks and tomatoes and teddy bears across the ocean, and every other boat we saw was pirates, chasing us. We made swords out of spatulas and whisks, and cannonballs out of apples. When the first mate and the cabin sprog were asleep, I could sit on the roof, floating under a majestic sky without another light as far as the eye could see, smoking a cigar with my rum. Moments like that, I was a billionaire.

~~When one of the engines stopped working~~ When we were flagged on the stern by a six-pounder crossing the broadwater, I sat Kai and Mikey in their lifejackets in the wheelhouse and told Kai

(I think he was six then) to press redial on my phone if I fell in and explain what had happened to the nice emergency people. Our trusty ship kept turning side on to the waves, plates were flying everywhere with the violent rocking, and it was all I could do to stay standing.

I was walking to the back to try and fix the motor when I heard Kai explaining things with all solemnity to Mikey, who was four. 'Mikey, if Mummy falls in, I'll go in and get her, and you call the ambulance, okay? Just press this button –'

'No!' I said. 'If Mummy falls in, you stay right where you are and hang on to your brother until someone comes. Don't move.' *Jesus, kid!*

Sometimes I was broke in everything but petrol for weeks, so we played car games. We would pack up a feast (probably dry cornflakes and the icky apricot muesli bars that always got left until last because nobody likes them) and go on Eeny-Meeny-Miny-Mo drives.

The rules were pretty simple: I'd drive until there was nowhere else to go, then the navigators in the boosters on the back seat would use E.M.M.M. to decide which direction was next, and we'd explore along the way. I could never disillusion them and let them in on the fact that we usually ended up back at home at the end of the day, because they would invariably start 'Eeny' on the right, so we only ever made left-hand turns. These drives coined 'We're not lost, we're on an *adventure*!', which translated to 'Are we on another "adventure" again, Mum?' if it looked even remotely like I didn't know where we were at any given moment.

While playing Eeny-Meeny-Miny-Mo, we could find abandoned

haunted houses and make up stories about who used to live there, or we could find a paddock full of unicorns. (I depended on my sprogs to tell me where the unicorns were, obviously, because growed-ups can't see unicorns.) Once we found a dragon's nest – a burnt cow carcass – so we knew that there were dragons about. I almost had them convinced that horses that wore rugs were zebras in disguise, and that the only way to tell the difference was to listen to their hoof-beats. Both of my sprogs are now excellent zebra trackers, should you ever need to hire one, by the way.

Driving at night, they would help me find the highest of all high points to get to, and it was just close enough to the moon that I could stand on the bonnet of my beat-up Ford station wagon and get them some moonrocks/car park pebbles.

~

Returning from one of these trips, we found an Emma. Our Emma's big old clunker car had broken down on the side of the road, and I stopped to help. I wasn't much help, but it was friendship-at-first-sight, and we ended up back at our house, drinking tea, playing my ancient piano in the shed and singing Billy Joel songs at the top of our lungs until 2am.

Emma immediately understood moonrocks and dragon hunts and why we had a semi-permanent pillow fort in our lounge room to defend against a likely invasion of the Spanish Armada. She spoke to Kai with the presumption that he would understand her like a growed-up, right off the bat, and he loved her for it.

On Emma's coffee table sat a fascinating collection of shells and stones and a funky oil/water novelty thingy that admittedly were the main reasons the kids liked visiting her place, but she was quite definitely a kindred spirit, and we kept her.

Emma rescued me plenty of times in turn. Not just as an emergency shoulder to bend or an ear to cry on, or someone to go fishing with – who already knew that we wouldn't want to catch a fish and hurt it – but also as tangible consistency. Nearly twenty years on, and she still lives in the same house and has the same phone number that we all know by heart, because she is etched onto it.

She has been the unchanging permanence around which we can revolve, the anchor that our little boat swings about, even if we don't speak and she doesn't know it.

~

For a time, I worked weekends at a 24-hour call centre in Sydney, two hours away from home, for a boss who would let me squish all my shifts together while my babies spent the weekend with Grandma or Nanny. It was a hard slog, but it meant that I didn't have to spend $100 on petrol and twenty hours a week commuting, and I got to spend weekdays with them. It wasn't a bad option for a single mum, even if it meant that I spent Mondays zombie-tired.

But one fateful Monday morning, after I'd driven home from work, picked the sproggets up from Grandma's house and taken Kai to kindy, I lost a bit of time and found myself waking up at my computer, a keyboard imprint on my cheek, to the *beepbeepbeepbeepbeep* of a continuously pressed letter key. 'Oh my god! Mikey!'

My heart did that flippy thing that it does when you can't immediately see your three-year-old, and you imagine every terrible fate all at once and play a full saga of a funeral followed by your subsequent arrest for child neglect and entry into jail, right up to becoming the prison kingpin who runs the contraband import business – all inside of three seconds in your head.

I came out of the bedroom, and a small piece of me died to see a dozen sets of little white powdery footprints in the hallway between the kitchen and the lounge room.

I followed them and just sank to my knees with a sob at the destruction. My baking pantry had exploded.

Flour covered every surface. Piles of it rested even on the tops of the light switches like window ledges on a Christmas card. And how the hell does a three-year-old get flour on a ceiling fan? Oats were stuffed into the VCR. Every cushion had been pulled off my beautiful sofa, and a big puddle of BBQ sauce was dripping down the side of one seat. Treacle handprints on the TV. Nuts. Currants. Desiccated coconut. Icing sugar. Brown sugar. White sugar. Glucose syrup. Rice. Milo. The place stank like warm, wet yeast. A sticky mess of caramelised brown sugar on the carpet had a wet dishcloth sitting in the middle of it – I can only assume that Mikey had tried to clean it up for me.

I called Emma, bawling incoherently down the line, 'The little monster ... *gack* ... he's killed ... *sob* ... my house ... *yarrrrg!*'

Like an angel of mercy, she showed up half an hour later with a vacuum and a bucket of cleaning products.

This was before the age of internet-shaming. In a messed-up perpetual competition, most parents carefully concealed any hint of evidence that their children might be less than angelic, so this event contributed to the weight of teenage single mother stigma in my mind. I felt utterly incompetent and alone. Normal people's sprogs didn't do things like that. Normal people could have actual metal knives in the kitchen and not have to padlock their makeup bag to avoid a repeat of the great Stayfast™ lipstick mural of 1999.

Treasure it, though, while it lasts.

Lately, I haven't had to worry about furniture being destroyed, and I'm not plagued by the need to constantly plug up the groaning dyke that holds back the mess. Now, I can have a Chesterfield buffalo hide sofa – my pride and joy, loved only slightly less than the matching wingback chair.

But my sprogs never sit on it with me. My baking pantry can be left unlocked and full of every ingredient I could ever need, but they never bake with me. When I play pirates in the pool with noodle swords, the only landlubber around to capture is the dog. I stand outside their locked teenage/young adult doors and knock for them to come and play with me. Occasionally, they slither out of their dank caves, hissing at the bright sunlight until I throw enough food and money at them. Then they withdraw like Vincent Price, chased by morning back into his batty mansion.

My head knows it's inevitable that they become more independent and need me less, that if my sprogs don't need me then it probably means that I've done my job, but it makes me sad to think that they don't see unicorns and dragons anymore, and that when they hear hooves, they've stopped thinking 'zebra'.

Dear Em,

Dude, this is my book. How wild is that? I've been saying things like, 'I have a call from my editor.' And, 'My publisher said …' All the while cracking up with laughter at how surreal it sounds. My publisher won't let me call it Only Pretentious Wankers Write Memoirs, though – I already asked.

Anyways, no story about our family would be complete without you. Friends who you can call after years of absence and just pick up where we left off, who still love us even after witnessing us cry snottily during our lowest lows, and preen – and strut obnoxiously during our highest highs – are as rare as wonky hens' faces, never mind their teeth.

I've been tempted so many times through this chapter to waffle on with something clichéd like 'We were rich in what mattered' or 'Money can't buy happiness' (barf) but screw that – if we can make that much fun out of less than nothing, what could we have done with resources? You and I, we'd have changed the world! Or at least prettied it up some.

As cool as it is, though, will this be the best thing I'll ever do? Am I going to be a grey-haired sad prat who looks for opportunities to casually insert this achievement into the conversation, like Buzz Aldrin telling everybody that will listen that he's been to outer space? Is this my outer space? I'll say, 'That's just like that anecdote I wrote about in my book … Oh yes, that's right, I'm a published author, you didn't know?' And when I'm leaving copies of this book lying around my guestroom, carefully hidden under piles of other books by legitimate authors (for visitors to stumble upon when they're nosily examining my shelves), how do I get TIME *magazine to write an endorsement for the cover so that I can insert this into my success montage?*

Will I still feel the same way about what I've written in ten years' time? Probably not, about a lot of things. I don't even feel the same about some of these words a few days after I've pounded them out on my keyboard and fallen asleep with my face in a bowl of half-finished muesli because I'm trying to write it and finish my degree.

It's been one of the hardest things, that's for sure. How do you take a snapshot of your family and your relationships and your children, and immortalise them in literature? They're constantly growing and changing (some changes more drastic than others, that's true), and I can't even get them to pause a moment for a photo. You should see how not-still they stand for a memoir.

Here's to loving friends, ever-unchanging in the fundamentals. We love you. We miss you.
Y, K & M

3

Not exactly a parenting savant

DROPPING YOUR BABY off for their first day of pre-school is usually a traumatic, teary event for all involved. It's a fairly standard parenting cliché.

But Kai was easy enough – gregarious and adventurous, he toddled in eagerly, tiny body disappearing behind a backpack big enough to fit him in it (I know this to be true because he tried it). He'd seen *Sesame Street*, so he had this shiz covered. Though, he was a little disappointed by the lack of puppets and spontaneous singing for a while.

By the end of kindergarten, I was banished from picking him up from his classroom because I was cramping his style, but sometimes he did let me wave at him from the gate.

Both of my sprogs have always been fiercely committed to their independence – 'No, Mummy! I can do it my*SELF*!' – but Mikey took this to extremes. When it was his turn to start pre-school, I was careful to explain that he was a big boy now and that his teachers would look after him because Mummy wasn't going to be there with him. That's just what you do, right? You prepare them for separation. And he'd watched me drop Kai off at school for two years – he knew the drill.

I parked the car, and he jumped out of his belt and leaned through between the front seats to kiss me goodbye, as he'd seen his sibling do a thousand times. But as I was reaching down to undo my seatbelt because I had to go inside to sign him in, he heard the click and his face just crumpled. 'NO, Mummy! You promised you would go AWAY!' He was inconsolable. He didn't want to hear explanations of sign-in sheets and safety procedures. He just wanted me to bugger off.

Every other parent was there having a touching exchange with their beloved offspring, who was crying delicate movie rivulets of tears because the thought of parting was too much to bear. 'Let's have one last reassuring hug, darling, then you can go with Miss Jennifer and I'll see you this afternoon.'

Mine, meanwhile, was screaming great gulping shuddery sobs, like I was killing him, because he thought I was going to *stay*.

He calmed down eventually, after I'd promised faithfully that I would, in fact, go away as soon as I'd signed the paper and put his bag on his hook. 'No? You can do that yourself? Can you find your name? Okay, okay! Of course you know your own name!' And I crossed-my-heart that I wouldn't come back until at least four o'clock, so that I didn't interrupt him getting to eat his lunch out of his new lunchbox. Stick-a-needle-in-my-eye that he could stay there all day *AND* come back first thing tomorrow, and I would go far away then too.

Geez. Phew. It wasn't until I'd been pushed out the door by the fraught staff and got back to the car that I began to miss him. My babies were all-growed-up, and I was going to be alone *all* day! *I didn't cry though. Nope. I didn't. Oh, shush!*

The routine of picking up and dropping off the sprogs settled down after that. I got used to it, but I don't think I ever got much better at it. I felt an unspoken dread every afternoon, and when Guy came along, he felt the same. We were mutually afflicted by not fitting in with the P&C crowd.

~

I met Guy when I was seventeen – at a Salvation Army youth group, funnily enough. For all my objections to the Salvos' doctrine and policies now, that group was a welcoming place for lonely misfits to meet and look after each other, and Guy and I found some much-needed community there. We struck up a light-hearted friendship, then lost contact for a while – he went off to sea to do his cadetship, and I went off to give birth to Mikey and raise my kids.

Guy sent me some funny letters for a while, but we were both from, and in, very different worlds. I want to make a ships-in-the-night analogy here. It'd fit, but it'd be way too corny, so I'll just put the suggestion out there, and you can take the blame for your own hokey mental picture, okay?

When Kai was five and Mikey was three, I found an old address book with Guy's number and love hearts doodled around his name – doodled ironically, which made me smile and pick up the phone to see if he still had the same number.

The actual year we got together is disputed in our crappy memories. There's a clue: when Guy came for dinner the first time, Mikey answered the door, held up four fingers and said, 'I'm number four. What number are you?' and demanded to know Guy's age on fingers before he'd let him in. As clubhouse passwords go, that's one of the easier ones we've had. Guy was lucky.

This would seem to set a pretty definite anniversary year, except that until he was about ten, Mikey would always round his age up. Being 'three and a half' was the same thing as being 'nearly four', and everybody knows that 'nearly four' is damn near as good as officially four. So if we're taking the sprogget's word on historical accuracy for the chronicles of us, then he was three.

Anyway, Guy had dinner with us that night, and then pretty much just didn't leave. Nobody minded.

As catches go, if we're going to perceive two people falling in love and joining families in a mercenary way, he was a good one. He had a stable job and no drug habits, and he wasn't malicious or aggressive. I had a fridge with beer in it, and a motorbike carefully taken apart and laid out in pieces in my lounge room. And I adored Guy's beloved dogs. It was never an especially passionate or cerebral match, but we were kindred spirits and our affection was deep. Even now, he is still the best and kindest man I have ever met.

I'm sure his parents must have had their reservations about his insta-family with a young mum, but they were always gracious and welcoming, and they have my undying devotion for being so lovely to my sprogs.

~

Guy's dogs had no qualms about living with new humans. Stinky and Molly adopted us right away, and you wouldn't have known that they'd lived anywhere else. They were mini foxy crosses with matching tan-and-white colour schemes, but Stinky was crossed with a whippet, so he was all skinny legs and teeth, and Molly was crossed with something unknown, and she was all roly-poly body and kissy tongue.

Stinky became my vigilant protector, though it was like loving a devoted cactus. If I put my plate down anywhere in the house, he would sit next to it and growl at anybody or anything that tried to touch it. If I was lying in bed, he would curl up in a tiny ball behind my knees (truly, I haven't been able to straighten my legs in fifteen years) and growl if he heard anybody, even Guy, approaching.

Molly became Mikey's long-suffering teddy bear. Every night

before bed, he would drag her off to his room for snuggles. She always had such a pained, patient look on her face as he took her, but she would wait until he was fast asleep before she snuck back out, careful not to wake him. Nanny from Peter Pan had nothing on our Molly.

She was fascinated by froggums: a huge population of green tree frogs, of all sizes, would congregate on our big wrap-around verandah at night to munch on the bugs that buzzed around the light. Molly would sit and stare adoringly at a froggum until the temptation overcame her – she would have to squeeze it to make it squeak ... '*Molly!*' She'd hang her head in shame. Her other favourite game was sneaking up on a frog and nudging it gently with her nose until it hopped so that she could sneak up on it again. Rinse, repeat. She could walk a frog clean across the yard, half a foot at a time.

Both dogs lived long, happy lives. Molly died at fourteen, and Stinky just a few months ago at more than seventeen. It has definitely been a year of changes.

~

Some of our favourite family in-jokes are based on social despair.

For a while I lived in an area infamous for being something of a ghetto of housing commission homes and low-income families. Guy and I went to, of all things, a wine tasting at my neighbour's house, where a particularly loud woman had sampled some cardboardeaux before she came and was determined to tell the entire room all her drinking stories. At one point she guffawed and bellowed in the middle of a tale, proclaiming, 'How am I supposed to know? I'm not the Pope of England, yanno!'

Guy and I snorted into our plastic pill-cups of cheap old grape juice, and it just stuck with us forever:

'What's for dinner?'

'How am I supposed to know? I'm not the Pope of England, yanno!'

We had a similar sense of humour, he and I.

The first time that Guy took me to meet his parents near Lara, in Victoria, they thought it would be sweet if we went for a drive to show me his old stomping grounds. I knew that we came from pretty different backgrounds, but I had no idea *how* different until I saw his school – a well-known school for the children of Melbourne's poshest that I'm not going to namedrop. Just having that school on your resume is enough to open doors. He mentioned as we drove into the grounds that the school had been irked at people (i.e. the general public) driving through the campus, so they'd bought the road.

They *bought* the road.

My schools had been the kinds where they'd have cake stalls for three years and hold the local Rotary Club hostage to erect a sun shade over the playground. Maybe if we were really lucky, we'd get a water bubbler too. Whereas this school bought the road to keep riffraff like me from accidentally stumbling into their way. (Okay, yeah, I have something of a classist chip on my shoulder. But the grandiose turrets and the pretty stables in the on-campus equestrian centre don't do much to help the rest of us relate, yanno?)

Have you ever noticed the correlation between skirt length and the fees charged by a school? The hem hoitytoityness effect can be tempered by the uniform accessories, though. Do you have a proper tie or one of the clip-on dooveywhackers? Have you got an actual straw hat, or did you go with the synthetic straw-lookalike stuff? These are the important things to consider with education. Forget kindness and robust critical thought – does the school have gargoyles, damn it? And do they call former students 'alumni' or 'parolees'?

A while after my visit to Lara, I finally got the chance to take Guy for a drive by one of my old schools. It took all of twenty seconds to go past: taking in the unpaved bush carpark, the thick iron grates on the windows – straight iron, not wrought or even slightly ornamental, in a purely functional 'fuck-off' kind of way – and the straggly natives planted along the inside of the ten-foot-high chainlink fence with razorwire rings along the top doesn't take nearly as much time as cruising around fountains and cultivated hedges. It's always bedraggled native plants for public school gardens, isn't it? I know there's a lot of flapping about environmentalist programs, but we all knew they landscaped with those because they're cheaper and they require bugger all care after the ribbon-cutting ceremony to open the school.

If I'm telling this story around a dinner table or at a party, for some reason Guy always feels compelled to correct the slightest dramatic exaggeration on my part by pointing out that it was merely rows of *barbed* wire at the top of the chainlink fence, not razorwire. So, for the sake of authenticity, I will do the same here. I stand corrected – the razorwire rings were only around the agriculture classroom and garden plot, which are at the back of the school. There, isn't that a cheerier picture?

~

For quite a while we were renovating our first house together, which just happened to be on the edge of one of the nicer suburbs in Newcastle, New South Wales. It was a cheap deceased estate, nice little old lady and all that, so ugly as sin and neglected, but solid with some funky art deco features that we were really in love with.

We enrolled the sprogs in a little infants' school around the corner, further inside the boundary of the 'nice' suburb, and got our first real taste of the classist social warfare that underpins our education system.

Neither of us were really concerned about appearances. Our dodgy 1983 sky-blue Corolla, which you sometimes had to start under the hood with a wire on the solenoid bypassing the starter relay, looked markedly out of place next to the shiny Mercedes of that real estate lady and the severe black tinted BMW that belonged to the doctor's wife.

Our state of dress would vary according to the reno job we were doing that day. Three o'clock invariably fell in the middle of the messiest part of it, so sometimes we (individually when one person won the paper-rock-scissors wager to see whose turn it would be, or together when one was successful in guilting the other into coming too) would be sitting on the playground benches with the other parents politely trying not to notice the paint-encrusted cut-off jeans, slags of Solastic glue in my hair and three pairs of safety glasses stacked on my head. I always thought that Guy's giant shiny balding forehead looked adorable covered in plaster dust, but apparently I was alone in my admiration.

I knew just how our Corolla felt. Most of the women seemed to be having grooming and fashion competitions that my decidedly uncoiffed self was never invited to. Seriously, who puts on red lipstick and heels to make an 8.30am showing at kindergarten drop-off? I'm not okay with shaming people for their choices – just expressing astonishment that anybody is that together. I was lucky if I found myself wearing pants in the morning, and even luckier if I ended up in my own pants, as the idea of making conscious fashion decisions so soon after waking up is completely alien to me.

My wonky cupcake and soggy Honey Cornflake Joy contributions to cake stalls always looked a tad sad next to fluffy artsy angel cakes and magic vanilla slices, and I never really mastered the art of not jumping up and down like a lunatic to applaud when either of my kids got called up to be awarded a merit certificate at morning assembly.

~

Do other parents wince internally a little when the phone rings and they see the school's number on caller ID? Was that just us?

Sometimes it seemed like every interaction was a battle.

I got a call asking me to pick Mikey up one morning because something had upset him. I don't remember what – could have been anything. Maybe they told him that yellow wasn't the colour he thought it was or something. Anyway, they were struggling to settle him down. He'd worked his little self into such a state that I had to drag him out of the school with him screaming, 'You abuse me! *You abuse me!* Stop abusing me!' at the top of his lungs.

Mortified, I asked how I abused him.

With a dramatic wail and an extended, heart-crushing sob, he bellowed, 'You'll make me clean my *ROOOO-OOOO-OOOM!*' Much to my relief, of course, he'd clarified what he meant in front of the first-responder-trained teaching staff.

Or maybe my cringe became instinctive after the time Kai's teacher pulled me aside to express her concern about our home life. Kai had been recounting some seemingly disturbing 'Uncle' tales. She was worried because in his short life, he'd already been exposed to 'Uncle' James and 'Uncle' Adam and 'Uncle' Colin and TWO 'Uncle' Peters, et cetera! (She'd been making a list, you see.)

It took me a while to understand what she was getting at, and I nearly fell over laughing while I explained to her that they are all Kai's actual legitimate and real uncles that he spends lots of time with: 'Yes, they're a lot older and fairly rough, but no, "we have fights ALL the time" doesn't mean that they beat him up – they just like to shadowbox and play.' I managed to resist the urge to explain to her that even if they *were* all my lovers, it would still be none of her damn business.

School became a battleground, not just because we didn't know how to play the 'We've just installed a pool *and* got a flatscreen, but it's a shame that little Johnny will have to wait until Christmas to get his Xbox' game with the other parents, but also because trying to keep up a facade of not being bizarre incompetent misfits got to be exhausting:

'No, there's nothing wrong with Kai's egg sandwiches, Mrs Keating. He just says they taste better if I dye them blue.'

'Of course he has a jumper. I've bought three of them already this year. The first two were too scratchy, and he put the last one in the oven because that's how you make things warm.'

The teachers didn't get it, but I understood.

~

The small bookcase that my family had when I was a child held some treasures – birdwatching handbooks and dry maritime histories and such – but none so fascinating as *The Macmillan Guide to Family Health*. You knew that Mum was taking your feeling poorly seriously as soon as she pulled it off the shelf. It held magical powers that inspired her respect, so it was automatically deserving of my reverence and awe.

The bible could hold my attention for a while too. I mean, it has stories about talking donkeys and bears ripping children to bits, and a dude offering his daughter up to an angry mob to protect his favourite angel from being raped. You can't buy that kind of entertainment in Hollywood. And I liked the dictionary, too. There are new *worlds* awaiting bored and curious kids in the dictionary.

I always came back to the *Macmillan*, though. It was awash with brilliant words like 'epididymis' and 'phalanges' (try saying them out loud). The best parts were the self-diagnosis flow charts at the back: a labyrinth of symptoms to navigate that eventually, no matter what you began with, led to brain tumours or cardiac problems. 'See your doctor NOW!' it warned ominously.

Which is why, at the age of thirteen, I ended up with an appendectomy instead of a maths exam.

The trick to getting out of class and napping in sickbay is to fake a condition just ambiguous enough that it might seem serious to the barely trained medical eye of a school receptionist. Serious enough to warrant a lie-down, anyways. The ever-popular and vague 'tummy ache' is good, but give it an air of seriousness by pointing to the right lower quadrant of your abdomen, and then it goes a bit too far. Things got really serious, really quickly.

Thirty minutes later, my mother showed up at the sickbay door, looking worried. Damn. She *never* came to the school. Interrupting her work day was a capital crime. This could be bad.

Don't panic, I thought, *she'll just drop me off with Grandad. It's all good.*

'You should probably take her to the GP,' said the ever-helpful receptionist.

Geez, thanks lady.

Twenty minutes after that, we were ushered in to see our ancient and solemn family doctor. We got bumped ahead of a waiting room full of authentically sick-looking people, so I guessed that this receptionist had triaged me as urgent too.

I suppose that about now (okay, probably long before now) a normal person would have fessed up, but that person has never faced down my mother's wrath. Our GP, with all his grey-haired, oak-desked, leather-chaired intimidation value, held nothing to the 'Oh, Yol*an*da!' disappointed exclamation of Mum in full admonishment mode. I was sitting in Dante's eighth circle of hell, with no idea how to extricate myself.

Even when the doctor didn't ask me any questions, just drew a # on the belly of a person's outline on his referral paper and told my mother to take it and me straight to the ER (*Shit!*), going along quietly *still* seemed the lesser of two evils. It wasn't too long before I was being wheeled into theatre.

I was sure that a stern surgeon would be standing at the end of my bed to reprimand me when I came to, but no. Nobody said a word about it.

I've wondered ever since if maybe there was a little panic in the OR when they opened me up and found a perfectly healthy appendix. How did *that* conversation go?

All I wanted to do afterwards was shut myself in my room and die of shame. Every time someone looked at me in sympathy or brought me something to eat, I couldn't say a word. Apparently that kind of cringing looks a lot like convalescing after surgery, though, so nobody even questioned it then. Aside from the occasional truth-or-dare game answer (that nobody really believed), I've barely told anybody about this and still, to this day, haven't figured out a way to tell my mother. I'm thirty-six now, and I guess publishing it in a book is as good a way as any. Sorry, Mum.

4

Growing green from red dirt

GUY FIT INTO our little family right away. He understood silly songs and dragon games and that he should sit in the back seat of the car because my Keeshond was jealous if he sat in the front. We were four of a kind – the kind who understand that dogs are people.

And we all understood that a 'Pet Goat' ad in the paper was something to be excited about, not something to pass over with a shrug. So we drove for two hours to meet a not-quite 'baby' goat that we fell in love with anyways, even if she didn't quite fit on the back seat of our tiny Corolla. 'Move over, sprogs!'

Guy proceeded to spend $1200 building the perfect goat house in our small suburban Newcastle backyard. Luckily for her, most of our property was cliff-like, so she had a blast back there.

The kids thought that Guy was a wizard. While he was building, he nailed together some offcuts and made rough toy boats and cars to keep them occupied while he worked, and they thought it was amazing and were convinced that he could do anything. Their request of 'Now build a robot bird that can really fly!' quickly became our catchphrase for impossible or unrealistic tasks. Every time we thought up a new project, he would tell us that he'd get around to it right after he was done building their robot bird. This also led to much hilarity later on, when we tried to convince them that Mummy's doves were the robots that they'd asked for, and that Guy had just made them *really* realistic.

Meanwhile, the goat – Bo, as we named her – didn't understand why she wasn't allowed inside the house. She never made the connection between me chasing her out and the mountain of pebbly poos that she'd left on the sofa; and no matter how many times I freed her from the doggy flap in the back door, she would still push her curly-horned head through and get stuck. Most mornings, we were woken by her machine-gun *BAAA-AAAA-AAAAA* plea for help echoing through the kitchen.

But there was something magical about looking outside to see Bo curled up in a patch of sunlight and wavy leafy shade, cuddling with Kai on the thick grass and helping him eat his sandwich. She was a window into that sense of loving humanity that seems perversely present in all animals, while it's sadly lacking in so many humans.

Space is there to be shared. There are no enemies, just competitors for food. Small creatures should be nuzzled and licked, and everything else should be chewed in an exploratory way. Nothing is malicious, but instead serves the hierarchy of who obeys and who is to be obeyed, who should lead and who should follow, who should eat and who is to be eaten. These are the lessons of goat.

~

Bo died, but not before we'd been well and truly bitten by the bug. We knew that we wanted a life with goats and cows and horses. We wanted to create our own little utopian world where our chooks were truly free-range and the sprogs could roam, wild and unhindered. Where we could aim for self-sufficiency and stop participating in the inherently cruel practices of Australian commercial farming.

Guided by uber-cheap land prices, we stuck a pin in a map and settled on a southern Queensland property that shared a postcode with the middle of nowhere. Our farm was red dirt and eucalypts, watering dams and old-school wire fences. It had a tiny farmhouse complete with 70s carpet, picture rails and about half a foot of lino bench space next to the steel sink in the kitchen.

It felt like we'd landed on the moon, and it was perfect.

I could describe in detail what it was like to do an interstate move, buying and selling houses over state lines, transferring everything more than a thousand kilometres, adjusting our citified selves to the ruralest of rural settings, miles from anywhere, but that would be pretty boring (and my editor will yell at me for going off on another tangent in that way that makes her face get all red and her eyes all wide and scary). I'll skip it if you'll imagine Alice tumbling down the rabbit hole mixed with Dorothy in a tornado, a psychedelic go-go boots dance scene and the frustration of waiting for a thousand monkeys bashing randomly on typewriters to reproduce Shakespeare's complete unabridged works. It was something like that.

Our farm was a little utopia, or what a utopia would be if the word was actually used to mean 'perfect sanctuary', instead of 'stifling and regimented communist dictatorship where individuality is crushed out of you for the sake of maintaining the appearance of peace and harmony'. I guess I could have called it 'Eden', but don't even get me started on *that*. Find me a better word to mean 'perfect sanctuary', and I would tell you that this is what we had.

Life quickly settled like a puddle into a puddle-shaped hole. Kai and Mikey got used to being outside more than they were inside, and they came to understand that every inch of everything was there to be explored and discovered, while I resigned myself to the fact that red dust, red water and red rock meant that I was never going to have a white anything, ever again. Grass was no longer soft and greenish, but brown and spiky and home to a million biteys, and the sun was no longer an ally in drying the washing, but an ever-present sniper watching and waiting to burn us with seatbelts and hot sand.

This was our introduction to a world where electricity can't ever be counted on, where bread and butter are made from scratch, where it can never be assumed that animal feed will be plentiful or even available, and where water doesn't just magically pour out when you turn on the tap. Water not appearing might mean having to dive twelve feet down in a muddy dam to clear a pipe's intake, or having to shower with buckets while you wait weeks for a pump part to be delivered.

Guy didn't waste his grammar school education and engineering skills – he spent his time building and fixing and doing ... and also arranging and rearranging his shed so that he had the perfect tool collection. But because he needed to disappear to sea every few months, spending more than fifty per cent of the year away on bulk carriers in the middle of the Pacific, I got very good at fixing broken farm bits too, so he'd come back to find that we'd all used tools and put them back in the wrong places.

It was a harsh and almost bipolar way to live. The hardships were so very hard and the work was so much to take on, but the beauty and joy were equal to them. Like suffering frostbite while you wait and curse out the mare who's too stupid to realise that she should foal in spring, not at 3am in the middle of winter, then ten minutes later being covered in warm blood and afterbirth when she drops her baby in your lap. Or spending weeks clearing land and chopping wood in the blistering heat, to enjoy cuddling in front of the fire with a basket of warm, sleepy piglets a few months later.

When friends in London complained about a fifteen-minute tube commute, they seemed extra obnoxious – I tried to explain that my driveway was longer than that, but it just didn't compute for them. That kind of bigness seems a uniquely Australian trait.

~

It got even harder to do the school uniform thing when we moved to the farm, and the sprogs started dressing the animals in their clothes so that they could pretend to have class at home. If you've ever seen a line of goats in cardigans and socks, you'll know what I'm talking about. (I don't know what it is about socks, but even if I buy ten packets of them, all exactly the same kind, we never seem to have enough.)

I used to find things around the farm that I just could not figure out. A Smurfette doll and a Snoopy, tied together and dangling from a tree. Half a dozen Bratz dolls buried up to their necks in the clay at the edge of a dam with ribbon blindfolds tied around their overly large eyes, only one of them facing backwards. Finding broken crayons mixed in with the chook feed because Kai and Mikey wanted to see if it would make the eggs come out different colours. (Point of interest, it doesn't – but it does change the colour of their poo, which gaily paints the chook pen perches.) Kai had a bizarre thing about coloured food – my home-made bread had to be purple for a while.

It wasn't that my sprogs were unsupervised a lot of the time, it's just that when you're on a large property, they have so much more room to play. When their small world is that big, and you have heaps of other creatures to look after as well, you don't always know *exactly* what it is that they're doing. The detective work to figure it out after the fact can be interesting, like a mystery novel character following a psychopath's trail and trying to get into their head, only with very much less bloody mutilation because Kai and Mikey weren't actually psychopaths, just curious kids.

Well, maybe all four of us were a bit weird, and I think we made extra work for ourselves doing things the hard way, but we were deliriously happy, too. The sprogs learned a thousand skills that they might never use again – or they may go on to survive the zombie apocalypse. They both drove the paddock ute as soon as they were tall enough to reach the pedals. Being able to see over the dashboard is overrated, especially when you have a little brother to stand up and spot for you.

Mikey, especially, had an independence that warranted more than a lofted brow. He was five when I caught him wandering home from the back paddock, in boots and underwear, carrying a pair of wire-cutters and a spray bottle of purple disinfectant that I used to treat animal cuts. 'Mikey, what have you been up to?' 'Nuthin'. A cow was stuck. She's not stuck anymore.' 'You know you can tell me that stuff and I can fix it, right? You don't have to do it yourself.' 'I can do it. I'm big.' 'I know, sprogget … but come tell me next time, k?' 'K.'

It turned out that my little Mister I-Can-Do-It-All-By-Myself! had found her tangled in a coil of old fencing wire and snipped her free, then treated her cuts. Though, if you knew him, you'd know that the only surprising part of that was that he was putting the snippers and disinfectant back where they belonged when he was done with them.

~

All that space is dangerous for a bunch of potential animal hoarders like us: we soon ended up with a menagerie of horses, cattle, pigs, sheep, goats, ducks, geese and a white (and therefore red) peacock, Frank.

On one particular trip, I drove a handful of hours to Warwick in our old truck to pick up our new house cow. Somehow, I don't know quite how, the truck ended up loaded with Raindrop the on-purpose Jersey cow plus two accidental Jersey calves, along with Rambo the merino, a crate of ducklings, a pony and an orphan miniature foal. It wasn't until just before I climbed the hill to Toowoomba at dusk and turned on the headlights that I discovered the truck's alternator wasn't working properly. I pulled over and rang a doorbell, asking to use the phone to call for help, and I'm not sure which the poor Samaritans thought was stranger: the teenage-looking truck driver, or the sounds coming from the back.

I've always particularly loved animals. As a little girl, I picked up a dying vole in a field near our house and put it in the chest pocket of my stripy dungarees to keep it safe. Of course, I forgot about it entirely, and Mum put it through the wash – which left a stain, but the thought's what counts.

The first time I realised that not everybody feels the same way about animals was in childhood too, when my family holidayed in a caravan on a farm property. It had everything you'd imagine of an English farm, from a sty in the fence to a tweed flatcap on the farmer's head. There was a fox corpse on a mound of grass at the front gate with milk-glassed eyes and fly-blown fur – a terrifying sight for any child. I asked the farmer why he didn't move it away, and he told me that he'd put it there on purpose, to scare all the other foxes away from his chickens. (Now, in actuality, we know that with territorial animals like foxes, a dead fox sends a message that there's space up for grabs, and new foxes will be attracted and move into the area, but let's not spoil a piece of old farming wisdom.)

That was the dawning of my contempt for people who are mean to animals. I couldn't understand why the farmer didn't seem upset that the fox was dead, even if the fox was dead to protect the chickens. He even seemed to be rejoicing about it. *We're sad when dogs die*, I thought. *Are foxes so very different to dogs? They're like dogs, but with bonus fluffy tails and a permanent whimsical grin.* It made no sense to my squishy-vole-loving self.

All things must surely die, but the only joy in that should be that the life was lived at all, not that it suffered. This is a sentiment that my sprogs have inherited.

At the farm, they became used to sharing the sofa with dogs and cats, feeding a lamb under the table at breakfast and taking showers with an injured turtle hanging out in the bathtub. Tuktuks (chooks) roamed free, and Frank's soulful peacock wail sounded out as he mourned his bachelor ways. I like to think that this all helped build my kids' strong compassion, as well as their resourcefulness.

I did try three or four times to find Frank a girlfriend. The first peahen broke her leg after one day and waited until we'd spent $160 at the vet to die. The second took one look at him and ran away at Roadrunner-from-Coyote speed, flying over gates – the last we saw of that peahen was her high-tailing it into the trees. The third one hung around for a little while, then relocated to join a neighbour's flock. Their cock must have been better looking, or something.

We became geese ninjas the year that a goose nested on the patch of concrete in front of the feed room door – the feed room that I needed to go into three times a day. Geese nest for about a month, and it's a cooperative job: the goose sits while the gander patrols around and forcefully deters invaders from coming close. So for twenty-eight to thirty days, three times a day, Kai or Mikey would sacrifice themselves to be chased by the hissing gander, letting me squeeze past the goose with buckets of feed so that the rest of the farm didn't starve.

The four fluffy goslings made this all worth it in the end. If you've never snuggled a gosling, add it to your bucket list. They're fluffier than a baby bunny, and they use their tiny soft beaks to nibble everything. Then again, baby everythings are cute – and it's incredible how creatures that are so very small cause such a large ruckus when they arrive.

The doe who kept leaving her kid in a burnt-out tree stump long enough to forget where she put him was unforgettable. Mother goats do this on purpose to keep their offspring safe from predators while they graze, so the kid hides and doesn't make a sound, even when it's Mum calling ... but usually Mum is smart enough to remember where she put them. Our doe would run back and forth, bleating non-stop at the top of her lungs – like a maniacal MG-30 with a never-ending clip – until one of us walked over to the stump and tossed out the kid.

The goats were part of my great self-sufficiency plan. I made a giant batch of goat cheese, but the thing with goat cheese is that it's empathetic – it takes on surrounding scents and converts them into taste – and that's why people pack it in lavender or nuts or honey, but the only place I had to store it was our laundry. It soon became known as 'Mummy's Old Sock Cheese'.

~

For someone like me, it was reassuring to watch the myth that motherhood comes naturally to every female animal get heartily squashed. Some animals are just crap mothers.

If you're a piglet, there's a pretty good chance that your mum will eat you, even as she ferociously defends you against other predators. If you're a duckling, you shouldn't necessarily follow your mother too closely, because she doesn't take your size into account when she walks over cattle grates and won't even hear you drop through. If you're a foal or a calf, you'll occasionally get kicked in the head when your mum's teats are sore.

I rescued a litter of piglets from just such a mother. PeggyPiggie was a big black saddleback sow with an attitude, boss of all the other sows and our boar too. I didn't count on her dropping a cluster of piglets in the main pen so soon (a quick bit of trivia: pigs gestate for three months, three weeks and three days, and I managed to miscount it), so I gathered them up in a hurry and stashed her with them in a milking pen. As likely as you are to be eaten by your mum when you're a piglet, being eaten by Dad and a bunch of aunties is even likelier.

After two nights, when I noticed that nine piglets had become seven, I put them in a big basket when Peggy's back was turned, took them into the house and went to buy some beer so that I could feed them – no, not feed them beer, just to use the leftover bottles. At every feed store you can buy a $1 rubber teat that will fit the top of a longneck, which can be used to feed formula to everything from piglets to wombats. (Wombats don't need milk that late, they just like beer.)

For the first few weeks, piglets need two-hourly feeds. Which can mean that you're feeding them constantly, depending on whether you count the two hours from the time you started feeding them last time or the time you finished. Kai, being the eldest, often set his alarm to do some of the feeds to help me during the night, and we survived our first litter of piglets. As they get bigger, they need less frequent feeding, which meant we could finally sleep through the night again.

They were down to just one or two bottles per day, and we had rehomed all but one by the time Guy returned from sea, just in time to fall in love with the remaining piglet. Guy fed him for two days, then went around bragging to all the neighbours that *he'd* bottle-raised his piglet. If we'd ever bothered to get married, I probably would have divorced him then!

We kept that piglet, named him Sausage, and Guy set about building him a piggie mansion behind his work shed. All his favourite animals get custom-made mansions.

~

I did learn a lot of necessary things from Guy, though. Things that someone stuck on a farm hours away from anywhere should know. Most notably, the basic principles of a combustion engine: Suck > Squeeze > Bang > Blow, otherwise known as Vacuum, Compression, Combustion, Exhaustion. And a thousand other gems of engineering knowhow, such as 'righty-tighty, lefty-loosy' to remember which way a screw goes, and: 'Fuck! That's live! Don't stick that in there!' (An old engineering adage.)

One time, over the phone from his ship, Guy talked me through the process of fixing a telephone plug. It was one of the old three-pronged numbers and seemed simple enough. I had some trepidation about grabbing the bare wire of the phone line to twist it around the screws as he instructed, but he promised it was only twelve volts and wouldn't give me more than a buzz. Of course, when I touched it, my arm was thrown violently with a nasty *crack*. Mr Telstraman later fixed the phone properly and told me that electricity was bleeding into the line, making the voltage higher than it should be. This is why I have trust issues. (Note for the future: even smartypantses like Guy are subject to the Dunning-Kruger effect.)

We tried to learn to ride motorbikes together, which was harder for him because he was away at sea most of the time and couldn't keep up with practice for the licence test, so I ended up getting it alone. I bought a great little Honda and decided that it would look prettier in pale baby pink (which is, I'm told, the least-used auto paint colour in Australia, even taking into account diarrhoea green and puke orange). A neighbour painted my bike for me, but we told the store supplying the paint that it was for a fridge – because whimsical and frivolous home renovation projects by the little woman cost less than more serious legitimate auto jobs, apparently. I tried to feel guilty for playing the unequal gender perceptions to my advantage for once, really I did, but sincerity was hard to muster when faced with a $300 price difference and the sense that there probably would have been a $300 female tax on top of retail if I'd gone in to ask for it myself.

I rode that lovely pink bike everywhere. The best thing about riding a motorbike is that if you go fast enough around the curves, nobody can hear you yelling *'Wheeeeeeeeeeee!'* in your helmet. The drawback is that most rural Australian roads are rod-straight and flat as a pancake, so I had to plan weekend trips and go as far as possible, making a special effort to appreciate the best bits. The only way to ride down the steep and curvy side of the Toowoomba Range is with Wagner's 'Ride of the Valkyries' blasting at full volume on headphones. You can trust me on that, I've done the research: 'Bohemian Rhapsody', 'American Pie', 'Don't Stop Me Now', they're not as fun.

I took a trip to Byron Bay and Nimbin on one of those weekends

– there are plenty of curves on the way, and it was within reach of my butt's ability to withstand the dodgy suspension, though I've called the place 'Numbum' ever since. I pulled in for lunch and saw the best graffiti exchange ever in the restroom. Scrawled in purple texta: *Amanda is a slut!* (The ever-present observation of cultural shaming found on toilet doors all over the country.) Written underneath, in a more severe font and black texta, was the admonishment: *This is not the Nimbin way.* Which was followed by a meek and contrite answer, again in purple texta, from the Amanda-hater: *Sorry.*

~

One constant through all of our lives has been Songs of Nonsense. (You can keep innocence, Bono, we prefer nonsense.)

Songs of Nonsense are made-up lyrics, sung spontaneously to random melodies. Sometimes we recognise the melodies from 'real' songs, sometimes not so much. They're not thought about or processed or even listened to, really. But we all know them.

They're sung to dogs, or horses, or parrots, or babies – so you, dear readers, will probably never hear them. Which is a pity, because Guy has a deliciously smooth tenor voice that only they (and we) get to hear. I think he can sing Songs of Nonsense without feeling self-conscious because they're not passed through any kind of mental filter. Your brain doesn't bother checking with your self-esteem or your conscience first, it just sings.

Sometimes they're very rhymey, or a mishmash of lyrics from other songs, or sometimes even the words are made up. They're an expression of pure joy, or exuberance, or plain washing-upness. Or even sadness. Nothing expresses grief like a nonsense song. Sometimes they make bearable something that would otherwise be un.

I remember Guy singing wordlessly to the sweet Mollybear as he dug her grave. She was our precious round Mollybear. Noblest of noble floppy-eared bottom-wabbits. Loving licker of the wounded. Fighter of snakes and valiant protector from fearsome froggums. Courageous woofer of invisible woof-worthy monsters at front doors. Ever-willing sproggets' night-time blankie and dutiful snuggler. Vigilant bath-watcher and clean-laundry smusher. Ferocious chewer of duckies, foot-warmer, cleaner of plates, stealer of sticks, connoisseur of yummy rocks, bed-takerer and slurper of eyeballs.

How do you acknowledge *that* kind of hole in the world with silence?

~

Mikey liked the cuddly things and would spend ages sitting with baby goats and carrying chickens around under his arm, but Kai was especially fascinated by ponies and horses. He spent most of his time in the paddock, hanging upside down from a tree branch, seeing if he could drop onto his pony's bare back.

We weren't inherently horsey people – I'd worked with horses as a teenager, but keeping them is a different thing entirely. Stupidly, we broke our horse-owning virginity on a stallion. Well, I did.

I wasn't even supposed to buy a stallion. I was there to buy a thoroughbred mare. I had a wad of money in my glovebox and a plan. The plan part was that I was going to find my four-legged soulmate, a gentle first horse that would be calm and patient while I dipped my toe into the equine world. If you haven't figured it out by now, my plans never really go according to.

Buying a stallion is a *dumb* idea. Even a relatively green horsey noob like me knew that. They are notorious for jumping fences (as I learned the hard way), and there are rules about double-fencing paddocks for them (double the holes to dig in the concrete-dry Queensland dirt), not to mention the difficulty of controlling them while you're riding near mares that they haven't met yet.

But there he was. As I drove up the long driveway on the seller's property, the stallion met me at the gate and raced me along the fence, occasionally backtracking because I wasn't driving fast enough to make the game fun for him. He was fast-stepping as he waited, his proud neck arched like a chess piece. Thick, muscled shoulders, strong thighs – but with a brain like a big cat. Everything about him was strength and marble solidness. He was black to his boots, with white, feathered feet and a white blaze splashed down his nose, and I could *feel* him thundering across the earth. He was the living embodiment of every knight's steed that I'd ever imagined in every book I'd ever read, and suddenly I was Godiva. I was Guinevere. I was every goddamn heroine who had ever even stood next to a horse in my imagination, and my heart was jumping. To see him was to love him.

When I got out of the car, I didn't even notice the

pretty-stunning-in-her-own-right mare waiting to meet me in the round yard. A great bay lady with a sweet and gentle face who I would have been thrilled to meet anywhere else, but who was eclipsed by the shiny attention whore, now pawing the gate with his foot and snorting great huffs of dust in indignation at being ignored.

The hairy twit stayed there, doing his best to distract the mare as she was shown to me. The seller took off the longe lead, and she kept pacing in circles around him, held by compliance alone. Blind Freddy would have seen that she was the perfect horse for a first timer. Brilliant. I'd send the truck for her on Friday. We shook hands on it and stood at the gate to chat. There's a lot of standing at fences to chat in rural Queensland – I think it's the state hobby. It's how news (gossip) is passed around and deals are done: economies rise and fall at the farmer's fence.

In between giving me horse advice and bemoaning the current government, in what I'm still not sure wasn't a particularly shrewd move, the seller said, 'The missus is fixing up the kitchen, so all my horses have to go.'

'All of them?'

The stallion bumped my shoulder with his nose because I'd stopped scratching his face.

'Yeah.' He nodded towards the pushy gooberhead that he already knew I wanted. 'He's $3500.'

Oh. Shit. Any notion that I'd ever had of being a pragmatic and astute customer got smushed forever. I had no idea what I was going to do with him, or where I was going to put him. Or what the hell I was going to tell my hunnybunny when I got home. I just knew that a life without this stallion in it would be a sad, dreary affair. Stop laughing at me – you'd have bought him too. Would so.

I named him D'Artagnan, and Kai was besotted. He didn't care a jot that the fuzzy monster was a hundred times bigger than him and could squish him without blinking – every chance he got, Kai was out there with him. He wasn't the only one, either. Stinkyhorse, the orphaned miniature foal (so named because he had the same tan-and-white colouring as Stinky the dog), adopted D'Artagnan as his 'mother' and spent his days hanging around the stallion, sheltered by his giant belly.

The pantry's entire cereal collection disappeared the morning after I'd brought the hairy bastard home, courtesy of Kai, who had snuck out at 5am to take D'Artagnan a bucket of Coco Pops mixed with Corn Flakes. I had to start buying apples on an as-needed basis, too, lest they get confused with 'fruit we don't really want' because they'd sat in the fruit bowl for a couple of days.

I have a picturesque memory of walking out to the washing line to find D'Artagnan lying in the shade with Kai leaning up against his stocky, furry shoulder and casually feeding him sugar with a spoon, straight from the jar, while he whispered horsey secrets. I got cranky at the time, but that's an image I'll be smiling about in my rocking chair many years from now.

Less idyllic was the first time I looked out the kitchen window and saw my tiny, fragile, utterly fearless little sprog up on his back – no saddle or bridle, not even a lead rope. I screamed and dropped a plate in the sink and ran outside. Kai was lying on the stallion's back, casual as you please, his hands folded behind his head and his feet crossed up on that big, fat neck, sunbathing.

D'Artagnan didn't give two shits. My stomach was in the back of my throat as I waited for Kai's inevitable death-by-smushing, but the two of them were just nonchalantly chilling out as D'Artagnan grazed. Apparently it was much easier to drop onto the back of that walking armchair from a branch than it was onto Kai's pony.

Eventually, Kai learned that he could use Stinkyhorse as a ladder to get onto his big boonterhead guardian, and then there was no stopping him. They grew up together that way.

D'Artagnan settled into a life of gluttony and pleasure of epicurean proportions, maintaining a delicate homeostasis between time spent satisfying his stomach and time spent satisfying his dick. In five years, I never saw him come across a mare who wasn't waving her arse in his face within hours of meeting him. Horse foreplay is a violent, terrifying display of squealing and snorting and stomping, and he revelled in it.

Until he met Domino. She was his perfect foil. A mare with the same luscious black colouring. The same sexy muscled neck and shoulders. The same casual fall of thick fringe over her face. Though, she did have a large round white spot on her stomach – hence the name. She'd had a bit of a rough start that had left her pretty timid and head-shy, so she wasn't so much bought by us as adopted.

The herd – D'Artagnan and his harem of mares – were in the far corner of my large paddock when she arrived. Too busy flicking flies in the shade of a tree to notice the truck pulling in. Once down the ramp, Domino lifted her sweet head and gave a loud call that was answered by Lady, the dominant mare. And then doofus, suddenly alert, did a comical, cartoonish double-take in the distance.

I know there's a cliché of thundering hooves, but that's exactly what they do. You could hear him clear across the paddock, barrelling down on her. She stood, frozen, until he got closer. Then her whole body stiffened – *bugger that!* – and she took off at a run in the opposite direction. He chased her for three hours straight that first day, his neck stretched out like Pepe Le Pew, but where his body reflected the muscle-and-sponge combination of lazy indulgence, she was solid and pure athlete. He was no match, but he kept chasing her when he'd caught his breath.

That carried on for months. He won her over at long last, and they had an epic equine romance, but it was the hardest he'd ever had to work for anything.

~

In 2004 I had my gallbladder removed and, as Guy was at sea at the time, my mother – my not-at-all-animal-keen mother – came to stay and look after our ark for me.

With Kai's help and under Mikey's supervision, Mum courageously braved morning feedings, carrying the buckets of animal food that I couldn't – various mixtures to cater for various diets. She milked Raindrop and got the sprogs ready for the school bus. I think she even started to like the pigs and got used to tripping over chooks. For years, whenever we ended up overwhelmingly surrounded by ravenous animals at feed time, or dropped a bucket of horse feed in our laps, the sproggets would laugh. 'You look like Grandma!'

But there was no way that she would lead goats. About this time, Buck (our creatively named buck goat) and our dozen or so nannygoats discovered the lush and plentiful grass that grew along the road about two kilometres away, and they would lead Rambo the Merino out there with them every morning. (With a lack of other sheep, Rambo decided that he was a goat too and would follow them under fences, resulting in a flat-top that would have made the Fresh Prince proud.)

After a frustrated visit from the local policeman asking me to get the herd off the road, we tried to lead them back with a bucket of grain hanging out the car window. It worked for a while, but eventually I had to make the rest of the herd follow by leading Buck by his horns, very slowly, backwards for more than a kilometre, trying not to pop my stitches. Buck was a solid black Boer goat, and he stubbornly resisted every step. We must have looked a sight: me in my ugg boots and dressing-gown, dragging him along the roadside.

~

Of course, life at the farm wasn't all comedy and tribulation. These stories are just lively punctuation on an overall tapestry of desert majesty.

When you ask someone why on earth they live in the middle of nowhere, miles from anything, chances are they'll struggle to describe it to you. It's so very hard to articulate the way the world looks when you step off the porch at five in the morning, in the brightening before the dawn, and disturb the mist that hangs on the ground between gum trees. Wet, burnt eucalyptus smell clinging to your clothes.

Or the way Australian soil turns more red-gold the closer the sun gets to setting, the light making everything more vibrant than it was in the sleepy, druggy heat of the earlier afternoon.

Watching the sprogs squeal and splash in the dam, feeling the squishy mud on the edge between your toes. Condensation making every bottle of drink soaking wet on the outside, and the heavy mug of a hot day finally breaking with the fat-raindrop lightning relief of a late-afternoon summer storm. Even breaking rock-hard dusty ground with a crowbar, digging a hole to plant an apple tree on top of your dead dog. It's more *alive*, more life than I've ever felt anywhere.

I watched Australia itself nurture my children, grow my family and fortify our hearts. We built something incredible, but I can't even write that. Everything I'm saying here feels so inadequate a description. If you've ever thought that this kind of thing might be for you, then stop fucking about. Just go and get it before the cynical world swallows you up. It's the best thing we've ever done.

Granted, there were times when I wondered what the hell we'd done to ourselves. Digging out thousands of noxious harrisia cactus blooms before they engulfed our paddock and burning them on top of termite mounds wasn't pleasant, and dropping the snake that killed Hamlet (our great dane) into a mulcher was something that didn't not suck.

But there's definitely enough joy to make life on a farm worth it. Like yelling out for Mikey to close the gate on his way to the school bus as I had forever, only to have him come straight back and hug me around the legs and say, 'Mum, Hamlet's dead. He can't eat the chooks anymore. The gate doesn't matter.' Mikey patted my hand in the sweetest way and ran off again, leaving me snivelling on the top step of the verandah, marvelling at my loving and pragmatic little spawn.

Like stars. Real stars. Not the muted and fuzzy kinda-twinkly shit stars that you mob see a few of from the coast, but the kind of stars that fill more than their own side of the horizon. The vast and endless streak of Milky Way, like a violent break across an outdoor ceiling. If you lie in just the right way in an open paddock, you can make it seem as though you're floating among them – not looking up at them, but falling, down into an abyss – to trick your cerebellum into forgetting that you ever had arms and legs at all, never mind where they are now. Or better still, if you and your sprogs lie on a trampoline with doonas and pillows and hot chocolate, the stars make the perfect nightlight for scary stories.

We farmed this painfully beautiful place through some good years and ended our run with years of drought. Fighting to keep water and struggling to find stock feed, during some of the driest years that Queensland has seen, tested us like nothing else.

~

I think the last straw for us was Dolly – poor darling Dolly. She was a huge Clydie mare that I'd found half-starved in a builder's paddock in Brisbane. A sight to make anybody's heart ache. She was in a flooded one-acre lot, along with her brother, a third pinto horse, a couple of minis, some sheep and a llama. She wore her skin like a too-big coat hanging off her gaunt frame, and her tail had been chewed on by the other hungry animals that she lived with: so hungry, they had started to eat her.

I brought her home, and we fed her up, fixed her feet (twice the length they should have been) and tidied her tail (half the length it should have been). I spent ages putting on a daily poultice to clear up big pus-filled cysts on her heels from where she'd stood in water too long.

Six months of solid feeding, and she filled out nicely and started acting like a horse again. Through it all, she'd been singularly sweet and gentle, and had become a fast favourite with Kai. He came into the house one day, holding a giant Clydie halter and a bridle that trailed on the ground because it was longer than him. 'Mum, can I ride Dolly?'

I didn't know. I had no idea if she was broken in – but she was so placid, I couldn't imagine her being anything but lovely. 'You should probably wear a helmet, kiddo. It's a long way to fall.'

I popped a bit into her mouth, and she didn't even blink as I fastened the bridle on. That was a good sign, but given that she was more than eighteen hands high (translated into non-horsey English: bloody tall!) it was something of a job for Kai to reach it. He had to climb on my shoulders to sit on her lofty back, and I held the lead tight, just in case. You never know.

We walked around in a circle with me leading, and she seemed fine.

'*Muuuuuum!* Let me go! She's okay.' Kai was his usual intrepid self.

So I tentatively unclicked the lead rope and marvelled as he trotted her beautifully down the driveway and all the way back again to come to a perfect halt in front of me. Miss Dolly didn't put a single hoof wrong the whole afternoon – you'd have thought she'd been doing elite dressage her entire life instead of entertaining building clients' kids on an industrial estate.

We had already loved her, but that moment was like lifting the hood of the faithful budget family car and discovering a Maserati engine. It was hard to get Kai away from her after that. The gentle giant – who was so polite that you could fence her in with a knee-high picket, and she would still wait for you to open the gate to let her through – loved him back just as hard, following him to and fro. She wouldn't even move for anybody else, but Kai she adored.

Near the end of our time on the farm, the summer of 2007, we had a six-week stretch of absurdly hot days. The mercury didn't budge much below forty, and as the culmination of years of Big Dry, everything suffered. Feed was so scarce that people started trucking it in from Victoria, and others preferred to cull their stock rather than watch it starve. I had my name on a waiting list for big round bales of hay, at near double the price I'd paid the previous year. But when it was finally delivered, it was just straw with weeds and no nutrients at all. No point putting that in the paddock. I complained to the store owner, who had the chutzpah to say, 'Beggars can't be choosers,' and shrug. I got cranky at him, and then we had to buy our hay elsewhere. (Far away elsewhere. Guy wasn't happy.)

One stinking afternoon at about two, I looked out the window and noticed that Dolly had dropped in the paddock in full sun. I ran out, fearing the worst, but she was still alive.

Barely. I had no idea how long she'd been lying there, but nothing can survive long in that kind of sun at the height of the day, and she was weakened from the years she'd spent undernourished (she was good and fat again by then, but constitution never really returns to good-as-new after a certain point). I threw a halter on her and tried to get her on her feet. Kai stood off to the side with apples, futilely trying to tempt her. I knew that she couldn't really hear him, but I couldn't bear to say anything. We tried for ages – hours.

My right hand was in a cast because I'd slipped and broken a metacarpal a few weeks before. It just crumbled away from my arm as I tried desperately to pull her up, and I could feel the bone break again. We just collapsed together, me and Kai clinging to Dolly's enormous neck and sobbing. Her eyes were rolled back in her head in delirium, and she was breathing painfully. The sun was going down on us like some stupid tragic metaphor as we sat there, trying to give her some comfort with our usual Songs of Nonsense, sung through tears – *Miss Dolly was a lolly who was sick, sick, sick … Dolly put the kettle on, Dolly put the kettle on.*

I eventually called my neighbour and asked him to come with his gun.

I don't like guns, as a general rule. I wouldn't have them around the house, even toy ones, but that time all they could bring was peace. Peace for this beautiful beast who had given my sprogget so much joy. She deserved so much better than this shitty end.

The neighbour arrived while I tried to explain to Kai what we had to do. He pretty much knew already – he was a farm kid. Everything dies, he knows that. It was just that this time, a piece of him would die too.

I sent him into the house so that he wouldn't watch it happen, and to this day I can still hear him screaming from the door: 'Noooooo, Mummy! Don't do it! She'll get up! Dolly, get *up*! Get *up!*' in gut-wrenching sobs.

He wouldn't speak to me for days, and I had to ask the neighbour to look after cremating Dolly because I didn't have the heart. It was devastating to find a foal skull in the ashes along with her remains a few days later when the fire had cooled.

That moment ended it for me, I think. When, not long afterwards, I was offered a job in a town an hour away, I jumped at the chance. As soon as I thought that the job would stick, we planned a move. We would leave our stars and our squishy mud dams and our early-morning rhapsodies behind.

I'll never regret that we went on our farming adventure. I

wouldn't take back a moment of it ... even that one. The things we learned, the childhood that the sproggets remember – all priceless. When I say that I can cook a meal from scratch, I know that I can cook it from the type of scratch that includes grinding the grain for the bread, and breeding and delivering the roast beast from its mama. If the zombie apocalypse starts tomorrow, I know that my family are the bravest, the most resourceful and the most resilient bunch of weirdos who I could ever hope to be stuck in a dystopian nightmare with.

But reliable running water is great too.

5

'As the twig is bent', or 'Thou shalt not do stuff'

EARLY SCHOOLING WAS something that came easily to Kai. He was bright and vivacious with a great sense of fun, the kind of kid who's really easy to be around and teach. If a little difficult for some people to speak to, because he didn't fit into the typical boxes they seemed to expect. He looked at things from surprising perspectives sometimes, and this could be tricky to keep up with if you weren't on your toes – or if you had rigid ideas about the way things were supposed to be.

That we couldn't just give things to people who needed but didn't have them puzzled him for years. 'But why isn't that man allowed on the train without a ticket if he hasn't got the money to buy a ticket, Mummy?' Though he grasped my explanation pretty quickly: 'Because that man is a member of the undeserving poor, and socialist policies like everybody having enough is a threat to the tax payers' misdirected indignant rage, a discontent that's fostered by industry moguls to distract people from realising who is actually stealing their money and keeping them trod down and under control.'

Kai was an empathetic soul, and I worried for him often because the softest fruit can be bruised the easiest.

Towards the end of 2008, I was invited to a parent orientation night for new transferees at the local high school that I'd enrolled Kai in when he finally came of age. We went along, excited at him reaching this milestone and keen to participate in a rite of passage for him.

But where I expected an information session about curriculum, assessment expectations and campus life, we (I and the other parents) were met with a two-hour lecture from a stern disciplinarian who was determined that we learn how beneficent it was of her and her staff to take in our nasty little hooligans, and how she expected the full cooperation from the parent body with her methods of handling such sad and degenerate examples of crotch spawn.

As a group, we parents cowered into our chairs and valiantly volunteered when P&C duties were doled out, in an attempt to pay back our debt to society after engaging in unauthorised breeding for our own selfish reasons and not to fill the understaffed workhouses like in the good ol' days. Thank goodness that this brave general was around to mop up the mess!

My mother made this pink dress for me when I was a baby, then Kai wore it.

Grandad built this go-kart out of an old stroller and some scrap timber, then Kai and his cousin Josh made him pull them around for hours while they giggled madly.

Still small enough to think that little brothers are awesome.

Sandpit critters. It takes six buckets and three trips to the beach to get enough sand for a sandpit – either that, or making tea for a week for the tradies working on the house next door.

Early school came easily to Kai. He was gregarious and precocious and loved everything.

Kai on D'Artagnan. One of the horses who we came to love during our time on the farm. That horse could look majestic as anything when he wasn't sitting on fences to knock them down or plodding along like a walking armchair.

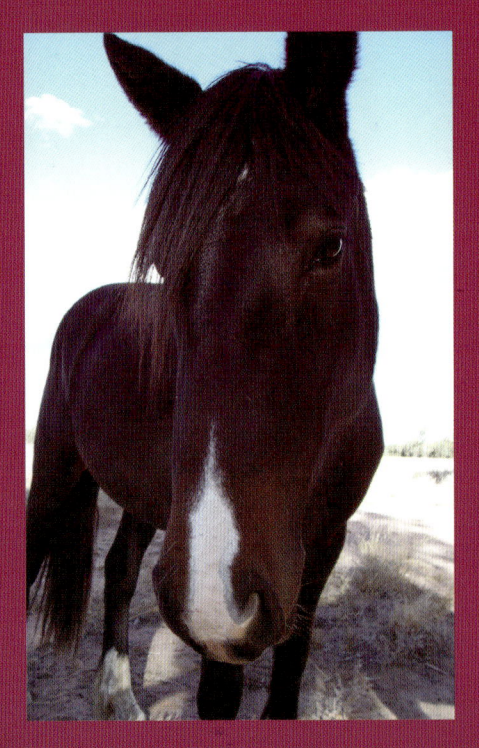

Kai and Mikey with Grandma. He complains about me taking his picture, but it's much harder to say no to pictures with Grandma!

This piece is entitled 'Blueberry skies'. A complete fluke of photographic awesomeness among about a hundred other blurry shots of nostrils and camera-drops while I was trying to take a picture of an uncooperative horse.

Lady. The herd's boss mare and my horse. She kept everybody in line, including me.

Kai's Seventeenth Birthday

Sometimes we miss the horses, so we have to find alternative ways to get our riding thrills.

Mikey & Kai. Teenagers with smiles – I feel like this shot should go in a museum or something.

For the photo-shy teenager who won't take pictures with his mum ... 'Oh noes! I don't know how the camera works on my new iPhone, sprogget! Can you show me?'

'Get the camera out of my face.' Another rare glimpse of a wild teenager in his natural habitat.

Bridesdude at Aunty Monique's wedding. This was before he came out, but nobody expected him to wear a dress because it just wasn't him. He was as he was and we loved him just that way.

Sproggets are exhausting! Kai often helps me with the kids that I nanny.

The picture used in the Retraction that went viral. Kai's expression is actually 'Geez, mum. Are you done?' because he was on the way to his formal and I was cramping his style by making all his friends pose.

I may be indulging in exaggeration here, but you get the general idea.

It was a portent of things to come. I watched Kai – who was unused to being automatically branded a criminal, waiting for his chance to strike – gradually fold in on himself and metamorphose from a vivacious and outgoing child into a sullen, silent stranger. I know that lots of parents describe this change in their teenagers, but I'm sure that Kai's shift in environment had a lot to do with it. I can't imagine being barked at and having someone suspiciously regulate my every teensy movement without it affecting my general mood.

While Kai was generally a well-behaved ~~inmate~~ student, I did get a call from Drill Sergeant Vice Principal Busttheirass about midway through Year Nine. Reportedly, Kai had been in central detention (the school equivalent of *The Hole*) every lunchtime for the past three weeks for the dastardly sin of refusing to colour in a small white streak on his leather school shoes with permanent marker because they didn't quite meet the dress code. The indignant teacher had been told: 'Sorry, Miss, my mum is way scarier than you. She paid $120 for these shoes, and she'd kill me if I drew on them.'

And I probably would have. Poor kid, there's not much he could have done about it, faced with such a dilemma. I wish he'd told me about it at the beginning, though. The thing about an early experience of financial difficulty is that the kids notice any money stress even if you try to hide it from them, and then they end up thinking that their needs are a burden and try to hide it from you in turn. Darling little bastards.

Running on the guilt of Kai thinking that, as well as not knowing that something huge was going on for him, I gave Miss Bythebook a serving over the phone. Thirteen-year-olds don't have a clothing budget, so if she had a problem with Kai's uniform, she needed to talk to the person who buys it for him, not punish him for something that was out of his control.

This was the beginning of a long war between us – the school and our family – about uniform. Kai was incredibly uncomfortable wearing skirts and would opt instead to wear long winter pants, the only 'legitimate' uniform option open to him on non-sports days, even during the stifling Queensland summer. Sometimes I could coax him into a skirt with bike pants underneath so that he'd be cooler, but eventually even that dwindled to nought.

Endless frustration. I had buckets of conversations with the school, but instead of being about his grades, or the curriculum, or his development – any of the things that actually matter – it was always about petty control issues, like uniform or his hairstyle not being 'appropriate'.

An absurd culture of uniform policing has developed in schools, where conformity to an arbitrary standard aesthetic is viewed as more important than academic achievement, or even the development of traits like confidence and compassion and pride in accomplishment. Is it truly such a heinous sin to have the wrong-coloured socks that a child should miss classes and be publicly shamed in front of their peers? Especially as the sock-wearer has almost no control over which socks are clean.

That's not to mention the rampant gender-shaming of girls in school uniforms – well, for anyone who's perceived as a girl and forced to wear the 'girl' uniforms. They're taught very early on that their thighs are disturbing sexual entities that should never be uncovered by a hem too many inches above the knee, lest they send impressionable young men the wrong message – except on Fridays, when they must wear a pleated sports skirt barely longer than their crotch. Are thighs less dangerous on Fridays? I could never figure that out.

Formal blouses and school dresses, cut to flatter a slender build with delicate darts and pleats, look frickin' ridiculous on kids who aren't shaped by the same cookie-cutter. Because that's just what young people in the midst of developing adult-sized body issues need: ill-fitting clothes. Even before we factor in complex body perceptions like dysphoria and gender disparities.

~

At the same time this was going on for Kai in 2009, I found out that he was being bullied mercilessly by a group of conventionally femme former friends for being different. He was just beginning to dip his toe into the waters of what initially seemed to be same-sex attraction, and they tortured him for it. General teenage stuff is hard enough to go through without the added weight of rural sexuality prejudice.

Heartbreaking as this was to watch, I have to admit that I put some of that weight on him too.

Years ago, my mum had given me a formal dress to put away for him when he grew into it, and occasionally, when I was sorting out the closet or packing away winter clothes, I'd bring it out.

The worst thing I ever did to Kai was force him to wear it when he'd 'developed' enough for it to fit. I got the idea into my head that it would be nice to send Grandma a picture of him wearing it, and I made him put it on and pose for a couple of shots.

The torment that I saw through the lens of my shitty cheap digital camera crumbled a corner of my heart, and I recognised his expression as the one I'd had myself, as I'd fought through the quagmire of stigma and bullshit, wanting to be who I knew I was and not the person that other people saw. I was bullying my own sprog, trying to make him into something that he hated. How does that even happen?

I apologised and deleted all but a couple of the pictures. I look at them now and then to remind myself of things I wish I knew inherently. I wish I always knew that his body is his own and that my attempts to influence what he wears or how he presents himself are manipulative ways to try and control him. I wish I always knew how to recognise the difference between my own discomfort with change and the things he's doing that are actually wrong.

Not that there's been much wrong to recognise. Kai has always been a good kid, eager to please and sensitive to the people around him. He's very likeable, and when he wants to turn on the charm, you can't help but love him – even when you account for the mother bias and use a control group. Any misbehaviour has usually been benign and comical, and I'm sure he'll be simply thrilled if I recount some of it here for your entertainment/education.

There comes a time in every contemporary teen's life when they discover the 'acquaintance' setting on Facebook and realise that they don't have to share everything they do on social media with their mother. While this makes it much harder for their mother to keep tabs on them, it can be got around with a bit of parental sneakiness. There's a fine line between letting a teenager explore their independence and giving them so much rope that they hang themselves – in permanent and public ways for future employers to peruse – so a bit of scheming might be warranted. (We have since learned all too well how easy internet privacy is to give up forever.)

Ostensibly, a fake profile for a teenage skater boy called 'Dwayne Pipe', quietly added to Kai's friend list when he was silly enough to go to school and leave the family computer signed in to his account, is one such method. It's the online version of letting your sprog roam a little to explore the beach, but staying close and watchful in case they need you.

It was lovely that Dwayne Pipe got an email to say that Kai had been tagged in a photo of him skateboarding at a park in a larger town, approximately two hours away, when I knew him to be visiting the local funfair instead. He had broken our cardinal rule of never riding in a car with a P-plate driver and lied about where he was going. *Umm-ahhhhh!*

He was grounded when he got home, and it must have killed him, wondering how on earth I knew that he'd lied. But he didn't say a word about it, and I wasn't about to tell him.

When he turned sixteen, I finally gave in and figured that it was time he regulate his own internet behaviour – privacy is important too.

~

One of the most disturbing attempts to *fix* Kai hit when he was about fourteen. He was singled out to participate in a SparkleyGIRLS Program (name changed to protect the litigious), which I hadn't heard of (and wish that I still hadn't). He was told that it was just a fun 'girls' activity, and the permission slip marketed it as a self-esteem building workshop.

It all looked fairly innocuous until I got to the last line. Written in a much smaller font: *May include some religious content.* Um …

I called the school counsellor who, according to the note with the school letterhead – the *public school* letterhead – was administrating the program. She reiterated that it was just a harmless and fun experience to help Kai build his self-esteem, and she insisted that while the disclaimer was there because SparkleyGIRLS was associated with a church group, the program itself wasn't religious. 'I'm sure they don't teach things from an evangelical perspective.'

Well sure, lady. Church youth outreaches don't, as a general rule. (I'm truly sorry that a *sarcasm* font doesn't yet exist for me to use here – you'll have to infer it from the context.)

Ms Counsellor, bless her heart, emailed me a copy of the

curriculum from the previous year's SparkleyGIRLS Program. So that I could see how innocent it all was, I guess. I don't think it occurred to her for a second that anybody would find anything objectionable about it.

The title or theme of it was about valuing girlhood (barf), and the rest described eleven weekly sessions. The first few sessions started out predictably enough: nutrition and skin care, how to do your makeup (not enough to look like a tramp, of course, but we gals have to be presentable) and how to fix your hair, et cetera. Yawn. All interspersed with various cerebral activities such as watching talk show episodes on DVD and learning how to properly compliment people on their looks.

While this is offensive in that it jumps, feet first, into the ocean of bullshit that reinforces to young women that they are vacuous twits who want nothing more than to look pretty and play with their hair, it isn't really anything to write home about. Rural children are bombarded with these messages from all sides: men do what's known as the 'real' work, while women 'faff about' in childcare, hairdressing and baby-making careers.

Don't get me wrong – I don't have any kind of issue with people who choose to become homemakers and raise a family as their main focus, and the dynamic of one person working for cash to support the family while the other takes on the not-to-be-sneezed-at task of domestic logistics can work really well for the people who choose it. And I certainly don't hold any disdain for those who work in childcare or hairdressing. My objection is entirely with the assumption that these roles should fall to women because of antediluvian notions that this is all they're good for and what they're best at.

Then there were SparkleyGIRLS sessions about how to properly set a formal dinner table, fold napkins and make 'good' decisions, like every well-behaved not-promiscuous future homemaker should. Scattered in there were declarations that all girls are princesses. Though if anybody actually treated them like a princess and set them up in an arranged marriage with an old man in some distant country to secure a trade treaty, their head would probably drop off in indignation.

But it didn't get *really* scary until 'Prince or Frog': a special session with a visit from a local pastor, a couple of male church members and the (again, male) school captains, where the girls had the thrilling opportunity to write down three questions that they wanted to 'ask a male'. As though males are some wise and alien diplomats worthy of reverence.

To cap it off, the last session was a visit from some local missionaries and a youth minister from the local chapter of JesusChristInfection (an evangelical youth group that I've renamed to use here) to inform the girls that they were made with a missionary purpose – not just to be beautiful table-setting appliances for their prince, no!

The feminist chunk of my brain was using a sledgehammer to beat an escape hole out the back of my skull, ready to knock heads together and rescue my sprogget.

After hearing, through an internet search and discussions with some other parents, that SparkleyGIRLS was apparently run by a notoriously well-known and well-funded evangelical fundamentalist group that targets teenagers with funky music, and reading about exactly how far the program reached in the public school system, I sent Ms Counsellor a reply email. Mostly to say that if Kai chose to join the program, he was welcome to and he had my permission, but that I was very concerned that a religious group was allowed to enlist public school students using such insidious means, as well as school resources and staff time. Even leaving aside the grotesque gender stereotyping and superficial content, it was clear to me that the program's aim was indoctrination and recruitment.

The response was as predictable as it was formulaic: shock that I would think such a thing about such an obviously well-intended and wholesome program, sprinkled with platitudes about nobody being forced to participate if they didn't want to.

I pointed out to Ms Counsellor (somewhat presciently?) that the program would be dreadfully uncomfortable for a young woman/young person-currently-identifying-as-a-woman starting to discover an inclination towards non-heterosexuality or wrestling with gender identity (which might, in fact, be one objective of the program and why Kai was selected for it, now I think about it – gotta nip *that* in the bud). I added that perhaps even straight, cisgender students shouldn't be sitting in public school classrooms being told that they're princesses created by a god in order to sign up more Christians for evangelical missionary work.

By the way, there's a version of SparkleyGIRLS for boys:

Strongness (not really called that). Its focus is, predictably, on reinforcing gender stereotypes from a male perspective and ensuring that young boys know that their purpose is to sign up to god's pyramid scheme sales team too.

~

Alright, the next little while reads a bit less like a memoir and more like a person's ranty manifesto, but if I may beg your indulgence for a few pages – this is likely to be the only legitimate platform that a random Joe like me is ever given, so I'm taking the opportunity to soapbox. Apologies in advance.

I want to make it clear that while my crankiness may seem aimed at 'religious people' as a homogenous whole, I really only mean to aim it at those who would seek to impose their own religious observances and values on others who don't share them. I absolutely recognise a distinction between these and others for whom spirituality is a private and individual matter. Big fan of those guys.

Understanding fully the notion of 'As the twig is bent', religious groups seem determined to encroach on public school grounds in any number of sneaky ways. As famously declared by Evonne Paddison (of ACCESS ministries) to a sympathetic congregation, her group sees Australian public schools – and their legislated 'rights' to access them – as a god-given opportunity to go forth and 'make disciples' out of children. To indoctrinate them while they're still credulous enough to take on the notion that they are born sick and need to buy the cure that only the church possesses, whatever the wishes or beliefs of their parents.

The latest strategy of such groups seems to be 'leadership' courses and gatherings. Which, to me, seems like an odd place to discuss sexual education and Noah's Ark, but they manage to slip it in there, counting on the fact that most parents are probably too apathetic to notice. We need to be paying more attention to the school-endorsed extracurricular activities our kids are doing and who exactly has access to them.

Even the yearly Christmas shoebox, which so many of our schools participate in now, has been revealed as a grotesque scheme to expose disadvantaged children in poorer countries to the 'message of hope' that they too are broken and should tithe to the church so they can live in paradise forever and not burn for being evil heathens. Parents and students fill a decorated shoebox with gifts, then hand it over in good faith (pun intended) to the organisation, which then tops it up with religious brochures and talismans before delivery, giving the impression to the recipients that they are beneficiaries of the church's bounty and not of the kindness of people who may not endorse the message at all.

Another infamous struggle over public school turf has been the Religious Instruction War (one of its main battlefields is the Chaplain Scuffle). Detailing this history could be a whole 'nother book, and it has been chewed on before by way tougher teeth than mine, so I won't spend more than a couple of paragraphs on it. For those who've somehow missed this going on: sometime in the late nineties/early noughties, 'Scripture' ceased being a harmless happy-clappy chance to do colouring-in once a week and started being a place to tell children that they are sinners and that they will incur god's wrath if they touch themselves. Someone high up in the food chain had the idea that making the program 'opt out' instead of 'opt in' – to take advantage of the general indifference of parents instead of getting actual consent – would give them access to more children. This started a tug of war between, on the one side, secular groups who advocate private religious freedoms and, on the other, a bunch of wankers who advocate their own freedom to religiously impose themselves on other people's kids.

Meanwhile, a conservative prime minister, who shall remain nameless, instigated a federal program by which probably-well-meaning but entirely unqualified christian volunteers called chaplains would be paid more than our entire flag budget (more than half a *billion* dollars at the time of writing) to hang about schools and 'look after' students, in lieu of actual mental healthcare professionals. This, by the way, completely ignores the 'there shall be no religious requirement for a government position' part of our laws. Eventually an incidental requirement for basic qualifications was added, but the religious requirement remains. It was challenged in the high court and found to be a naughty misappropriation of federal funds that pooh-poohed the secular intent of legislation, but hey, it's still going.

Given that these same governments have had a fire sale with education cuts and slashes to disability services, as well as to services for aged pensioners, the favourite vulnerable group that can't fight back, dipping into the public purse to support indoctrination efforts is obscene.

But even with all the loopholes, dishonesty and general sneakiness of groups with ideological agendas and 'cool' names to appeal to the young'uns, old hats like the Gideons are still being given open and unfettered access to kids. Mikey came home in Year Eight with a shiny new bible, given to him during a special assembly (endorsed and enabled by the school) where students had been told by a 'visitor' that they could find the answers to life's problems inside this book. The school, predictably (again), just shrugged, dismissed it as benign and excused it as a tradition – completely ignoring the section of Queensland education legislation concerning sectarian publications distributed in schools. (The general gist of that legislation is 'Don't.')

Then when it comes to sex-ed classes, fundamentalist evangelicals and their ilk lobby for control of the curriculum because they consider it best for teenagers to learn that the only valuable kind of sexual expression is that between two heterosexual people in a permanent monogamous relationship. This is profoundly disconnected from the reality of many people's lives. Fundamentalists hang on grimly to ideas of purity as a valuable mental barrier to prevent teenage sex. 'Virginity': the idea that a penis is so powerful that just touching one is enough to fundamentally alter and devalue a woman. One guess where *that* notion came from.

Shocking news: some teenagers have sex. Teenagers have been having sex since the dawn of time, and they will continue to have sex till the end of time, however uncomfortable parents are with the idea of their sproggets as sexual beings. (Our kids are probably just as disturbed to consider that their parents bump uglies too, yanno.) In the spirit of bending twigs to make healthy adults, surely it's best for them to learn about positive sexual expression, consent issues, responsible STI protection and contraception, so that they can choose when or if to become parents themselves?

Messages are sent out that blend ideas about shame and contrition with lessons about 'sinful' sexual behaviour, and this contributes to dysfunction on a much larger scale. It's not farfetched to imagine a teenager internalising the idea that if a topic is presented as taboo, then there's something inherently wrong with a person who is interested in it, i.e. they are curious about sex, therefore bad. And that girl in their class likes sex and expresses herself freely, so she must be *really* bad.

Sexuality is a fundamental part of the human experience, and knowledge about sexuality is not anyone's to withhold in order to control the choices and decisions that others make – even if that other person came out of their womb. Sexuality belongs to everybody, which means that everybody may determine for themselves who and how they will fuck.

And while we're at it, why not assume a state of impermanence and give kids some information about not only ending relationships, but also being civil and productive when dealing with former partners? The chances are pretty high that they'll have more than one significant relationship in their lives, so why not consider those to be transitional stages instead of preparing them for an 'ideal' lifetime god-sanctioned heterosexual marriage and then watching them berate themselves when that fails? A thing does not have to last forever to have value – ask anybody who's ever loved a dog.

~

There's a fairly recent initiative in Australia called the Safe Schools Coalition. Their sole purpose is to offer educational resources and support to schools, in order to make school environments safe for everybody, whatever their gender identity, intersex status, sexuality, religion or anything else.

Eleven out of every hundred Australians are gender or sexuality diverse (Human Rights Commission, 2014). This means that in a school of a thousand kids, 110 of them are likely coming to terms with same-sex attraction or trying to deal with not fitting into narrow binary gender groupings. Not included in that number are kids who live with parents who are in non-heterosexual relationships, and others who have gender and sexuality diverse family members, whom they love.

That's a lot of kids being affected by this.

That's a lot of people to send messages to, directly and indirectly, to tell them that they don't belong, that they don't deserve to feel safe and included and accepted, because they don't fit some people's ideals of what they 'should be', or what is 'right' and 'proper'. That said, even if it were just one or two students per school, surely they'd still have the right to safety and inclusion?

One of the main detractors of the Safe Schools Coalition seems to believe that heterosexuality and binary cisgender presentations are the pre-programmed default, and that young people are only 'corrupted to sin' (sin, also known as any identity other than heterosexual and cisgender) by the bad influence of evil adults who lead them astray with talk of condoms alongside lecherous (otherwise known as biologically accurate) pictures of genitalia in sex-ed classes. This particular group has gone to great lengths, down many avenues, to thwart Safe Schools.

A book is hardly up-to-the-minute news, and I know that things can change in the months between writing it and reading it on paper, but today I heard that some of the vital support services allied with Safe Schools have had their funding cut – and that one of the people who's been indispensable in supporting Kai through his transition has lost their job. It's very hard not to be angry about interference that's directly intended to impose one set of views over another.

To them I say: 'There is no "gay agenda". Get over it. There aren't any groups of gender and sexuality diverse adults meeting secretly in boxrooms in the back of bars, scheming and plotting ways to make otherwise straight young people gay and transgender, and to indoctrinate them to our cause so that we'll have a continual supply of fresh meat to exploit. (That's your bag.) We're not fighting and worming our way into schools because we know that young minds are easier to influence and that they're a ripe stomping ground to plant seeds or make disciples. (Again, that's all you.)'

People figure out for themselves that they have same-sex

attraction or that their gender identity doesn't match their biological sex. They've always done so, even immersed in ultra-conservative, hyper-stereotyped gender role environments. Even surrounded by heterosexuality, with bugger all exposure to The Gay Agenda™, young folk still discover their own diversity. As a society, the only part we get to decide is whether or not they suffer for it. Pretending that it's not there doesn't make it go away. Cutting funding to the services that support these discoveries and early explorations – in safe and inclusive ways, in order to mitigate the damage of growing queeriosity in a hostile world – doesn't do anything but harm the kids that the fundamentalists claim to be trying to protect.

Don't be mistaken: I don't doubt that the beliefs that often dictate these efforts are sincerely held and kindly meant, and that these things are done with a genuine view of what is to be valued as good. But appeals to tradition and the wholesomeness of an unrealistically idealised past aren't enough. We have the ability and forethought available to us to design our communities in a way that achieves truly secular standards, where each person may pursue their own happinesses without infringing on those of others (including ones that involve faith). We can't do this while we're basing the public good on a fraudulently objective morality to be imposed by those in whose imaginations it has been born.

The same effect is produced during discussions about non-heterosexual marriage. You can't legislate the formation of families. People will love who they love and breed with whomever they choose, despite disapproval. Families don't care if people think that they ought be or not. Sexuality and gender diverse families exist: they're not going anywhere. So, the legislation that these fundamentalists object to – the thing that they keep voting 'no' on – is simply to keep it enshrined in law that these families are worth less than theirs. To declare it civilly that these families are illegitimate. That their love is less valid.

'Oh, but won't you think of the children?'

These fundamentalists aren't concerned with the children, and to claim that they are seems facetious. They're arguing about the legal recognition granted to relationships between two *adults*. The rights of children to their genetic heritage is a different issue entirely – and, even then, rights to genetic heritage don't entitle a child to be raised by their dam/sire, or step-parenting would be illegal. The legislation about marriage applies to couples whether or not they choose to become parents. If the sole concern was parentage, then the sole legislative concern would be about parenting, and it would therefore give equal effort towards the banning of single-parent families.

The argument falls short again when it is reinforced that the predominant reason for marriage is procreation. Do these people also lobby to prevent the marriages of heterosexual couples who don't intend to breed? Or specifically mature couples (*waves to Fred Nile*), or other known infertile couples who can't fulfil that particular prerequisite? It seems that only 'icky' pairings are targeted.

The next argument involves 'freedom of speech and religion'. But when someone stands in front of an abortion clinic to protest at people who obviously don't share their views, they're not interested in exercising their right to speak: they're interested in forcing others to listen. When someone insists on legislation to force all of Australia to obey their religious views, they're not simply exercising their own religious freedoms: they're trying to impose them on other people.

Don't get me wrong, I know there's a whole bunch of sincere and lovely religious folk out there. I'm not trying to persecute anybody or deny them the right to believe whatever they like. But I do wish that some religious people would try, just for a moment, to picture how life must be for those of us on the other side who don't (and never will) share their deeply held beliefs. It can be impossibly hard to describe how strange it is to live in a world where, without those beliefs, the rules that others try to impose seem entirely arbitrary.

~

I don't normally like to see people use the 'it's not a choice' position in a discussion, because to me this implies that there would be something wrong with making a decision to identify with diverse sexualities or genders, even if it was a choice.

Take a moment to let the implications of the challenges that these sprogs face sink in. Who would deliberately walk this path? Who would set themselves up for this kind of scorn, vilification and rejection on a whim or because they think it's trendy? Why on earth would a person risk being thrown out of home, shunned by their family and friends, and endangering their education and career on a superficial impulse?

Consider how strong and profound a compulsion would need to be in order for you to make a similar choice, and you might get an inkling about how deeply a sprogget is affected by the way they feel. They already know, intimately, the potential consequences of being open ... and they do it anyway. This attests to an impressive fortitude and resilience. I don't know how to be anything other than immeasurably proud of Kai. That said, sometimes it's not safe or possible to come out, and sprogs in this situation are no less remarkable for their strength.

Being transgender can be devastating to someone's family relationships, career opportunities, social and romantic connections, even self-esteem and mental health. But the thing is, being transgender doesn't *cause* damage to family, social and romantic connections. It doesn't have any bearing on whether a person can do the job they're qualified for, and it doesn't mean that they're not mentally healthy. All the unique issues and challenges facing transgender folk (and indeed, everybody else under the gender and sexual diversity umbrella) are created directly by the attitudes and perceptions of other people. These issues and challenges are part of an external reality, not a result of a subjective cause.

What a person wears, which pronouns they use, whether or how they alter their body. Who a person sleeps with and how. These are entirely benign things. The other stuff, though – the stuff that is not benign, that contributes to a scarily high number of kids self-harming, suiciding, being homeless – we definitely have a choice about that.

I'm a secularist, which means that I'm a big supporter of people being able to practise their personal religion in any way that they see fit. Not because I see anything particularly important or worthy of reverence about religion, but because I hold personal freedom, bodily autonomy and self-determination sacrosanct. Everybody has an equal right to determine for themselves the best way to spend their time and use their resources, but not so far as it restricts somebody else's similar right.

These things, they're all connected: abortion, medical gatekeeping, voluntary euthanasia, gender disadvantage, homophobia, transphobia. The idea that one person has the right to tell another what is good and worthy, and what they should be permitted to do with their body, is at the root of so much argument between liberal and conservative, left and right.

If we're going to live in a truly pluralist society, then what one person or group of people values cannot be imposed on another, whether that group is the majority or not. Either human rights are universal, or we grant rights to one group that we keep from another.

~

So many people have asked me about what makes our family different, though we've never considered ourselves anything other than utterly average. The publisher who approached me to write this book seemed to think that there would be something special and unique in our story, something remarkable or extraordinary that sets us apart and enables the easy acceptance of things that have split other families into pieces.

Well, if there's anything at all, then I imagine it's this: our brand of Secular Humanism that values people and the things they do, and that values compassion and equality, self-determination and actualisation, along with the pursuit of knowledge and understanding and culture, without revering traditions simply because they are traditions. A thing is not necessarily good just because it has been around for a long time, and sometimes relics of the past need to be resigned to the past to be forgotten.

I've also been asked: 'How can you allow Kai to mutilate his body? How can you be okay with it?' (Ironically, this was said by someone who has previously argued for their own right to circumcise their infant son in accordance with their religious beliefs. Yeah, dude, you know who you are. Doofus.)

Okay, so two words in that question already answer it just fine: *His body.*

Bodily autonomy is a concept that says we have sovereignty over ourselves and are the sole arbiters of our physical choices. That's why a person in Australia can't be ordered to donate one of their kidneys to someone who would die without it (even though they have one spare), or why, even though it's desperately needed, nobody can be required or otherwise forced to donate blood.

Bodily autonomy is fundamental – the basis of all of our human rights. The right not to be raped or assaulted. The right not to be enslaved. I happen to like not being enslaved and regularly enjoy that part of our social contract, and I'm sure you do too. (Just as an aside, bodily autonomy is also why a person's right to say whether or not someone gets to reside in their womb is more important than that someone else's need to be there. And why a parent shouldn't have the right to alter their kids' junk to suit their own aesthetic sensibilities or to appease foreskin-hating deities.)

Kai's body isn't something that I get to 'permit'. Parents don't get to determine who their sproggets are, or what they do with their bodies and lives. We don't get to choose who they sleep with or have relationships with. We don't get to decide which career they should study for or what their values should be.

I joke with Kai about him being Me 2.0, but he knows it's a joke. Our children aren't our accessories. They aren't extensions of ourselves. We can teach them what we value when they're young, but ultimately everybody must live according to their own conscience. While I value solicited advice from my family and friends, I sure as hell don't look to them for permission and validation as regards my health choices. I've got $1 that says that you probably don't ask your mother's opinion on whether or not to get a new piercing or how to style your pubic hair, either.

Kai will make his own decisions about transitioning and his body. He will pursue his own happiness. No matter what that looks like or what choices it involves, he will have a supportive and loving mother who isn't just okay with him – who *celebrates* him, exactly as he is.

~

Half the futility I feel at trying to change anybody's hearts and minds is because I know damned well how hard it can be to change my own mind about something, especially when I'm on the defensive about it. I like to think that I'm reasonable and open to persuasion by solid logical arguments, but so does everybody else.

Most people understand that it's irrational to hold to a position when there's new information that contradicts it, but if you're already compelled to hold that position, then you're already mostly convinced. I'm not entirely rigid, though, so here are a couple of the reasons why I have a niggly bit of hope that others can change – enough, at least, to make me think that writing this damn book and appealing for change isn't a total waste of time.

The first reason is about eating meat.

Guy came home from a swing at sea and announced that while he was gone he'd given up eating animals. I was pretty put out. I mean, we'd always had a mutual love of critters and a mutual disdain for commercial meat production – you don't move to the middle of the desert to raise your own beasts for no good reason. But it was a huge lifestyle decision for him to make without consulting me.

I was more than a tad cranky about it. Pretty much everything that I knew how to cook had dead animals in it. I had roasted and marinaded and stir-fried flesh happily for years. I rallied and railed for about a month, pouting and carrying on about how much of a pain in the arse it was for one member of the family to have a different meal to everybody else ... before I admitted that I agreed with him.

I was a volunteer for the RSPCA at the time, driving the wildlife ambulance and doing simple rescue jobs like pulling ducklings from drains. Driving for hours to fetch a baby bird from one side of Brisbane to take it to be cared for on the other, and then going home to a chicken dinner ended up making no sense at all.

So, no more meat for me. (And, without trying to turn this chapter into a vegetarian love-in, my cholesterol and all my other health markers have never been better. Yay for kindness!)

The second of my mind-changing epiphanies went like this:

Years ago, I went on a date with a man who took me to his parents' Indian restaurant. I told him that I'd never really had Indian food before, and he thought it would be hilarious to serve me the hottest meals, knowing that I was trying to be polite to his folks. Ha-dee-fucking-*HA*, dude. I sat there sculling milk and rubbing my poor tongue with naan, my eyes watering. The next morning was spent behind the closed door of the bathroom. I decided that I never wanted to touch Indian cuisine again.

That was more than fifteen years ago. Then, at a cross-cultural potluck last year, someone brought in an array of Indian vegetarian dishes. (*I love you, Aruna, seriously: songs and stories should be written about your cooking.*) Holy shit. Indian food is feckin' delicious. I felt robbed of years of paneer kofta and naan! I was so angry with myself.

I know that I'm unlikely to sway anybody who is thoroughly convinced that being gender or sexuality diverse is an affront to their beliefs, but maybe there are some fence-sitters out there who haven't yet realised how much this stuff matters. It matters, guys, and we can't ignore it any longer – it's doing too much harm. Consider this your recruitment call.

Kai

I pulled a face at Mum when she asked me to write about my experience of high school. It's not something that I like to remember. All my memories seem to squish together and make one big abstract mess of loneliness and frustration and unhappiness in my head.

It all just seemed so petty. Detention for stupid reasons, and the insistence on conformity to completely arbitrary rules just for the sake of having rules. It's like school staff become so entrenched in the culture of the school, and in maintaining discipline and compliance, that they forget to ask why the rules exist at all, never mind considering whether they might be harmful to their students.

What does it matter if my shoes have a stripe on them? In ten years' time, do you think that my family or my employer is going to care more that my school uniform wasn't up to scratch, or that I understand respectful relationships and the worth of a person because I've felt valued and respected? School staff, are you empowering your students or crushing the soul out of them because they dare to make choices you wouldn't make for them?

But some individual memories do jump out at me from the mess:

The time a male teacher ignored canoodling hetero couples on the playground to single out two boys who were holding hands and humiliate them for their sweet exploration of affection.

Seeing girls lined up against a wall, like in a criminal interrogation, and watching each one while she cleaned her face with a makeup remover wipe – the teacher in charge sent those whose cloths didn't come back clean to detention.

On a free-dress day, watching boys run around in singlets, while girls who had dared to bare some sexy twelve-year-old shoulder to the Queensland heat were told to put on filthy jumpers from the lost-and-found box to make themselves 'decent' enough to play outside.

Having to beg a male teacher to excuse me from swimming because I'd just got my period and was embarrassed.

School felt like a warzone to me. A perpetual state of martial law that I knew I had to endure until graduation, when I could be free and actually start to live. I hid being transgender at school because of how hard it was just to be 'Beth' there: Kai would probably have withered and died, or reached critical mass and exploded. I don't really know which.

If there are kids like me out there, reading this, please hang in there. I know the 'it gets better' crap is silly, and that it doesn't help you in the here and now, but I promise you that it's worth the wait. I promise that one day you'll be able to live in a world where you aren't automatically assumed to be guilty of misbehaving, where you don't have to ask permission to go to the toilet, and where you get to decide when you speak and what you say, instead of having it dictated to you by someone else who acts like a fucked-up uniformed robot in a Will Smith movie.

    I'm okay, and it's okay to be you too.

6

Peddling Books

O for a book and a shady nook
Either indoors or out;
With the green leaves whispering overhead,
Or the street cries all about;
Where I may read all at my ease,
Both of the new and old;
For a jolly good book whereon to look,
Is better to me than gold.

– John Wilson (?–1889)

WHEN KAI WAS about thirteen, we opened a little new and used bookshop in our small town. I'd spent years trying to foster a love of books in my kids – without my tendency towards medical confabulation, of course. As it turned out, surrounding them with thousands of books, making them shift hundreds of boxes of books and forcing them to babysit me in the bookstore after school didn't help that cause. But it sure was an 'adventure'.

On the first day that I opened the shop, a journalist from the local rag came around to do a story on the latest addition to the bustling centre of commerce that was our 200-metre-long main street. We decided on some good comments to use in her article, and she asked me to pose with a book for a picture. I just plucked an art book off the shelf and didn't think much of it, until a couple of days later when I saw my smiling face proudly championing a red book with 'DEMONS' in bright letters. The book's subtitle – something like 'in art and literature' (truly, it was a fascinating book) – wasn't discernible. I had to rest my head on my desk at the realisation that I'd announced myself as the new occult bookstore servicing a town known for its pious religiosity.

It didn't help that the seemingly benign (at the time) comments she'd quoted – that I wanted to appeal to teenagers with my great range of fantasy fiction, and to children with a daily story-time – took on a sinister slant next to that bold title.

The town had a population of less than five thousand, but more than a million separate places of worship for various denominations, as well as two religious schools (and I kid you not, we were within a few hundred kilometres of an *actual* Jesus reincarnation), so it wasn't long before I had visits from concerned clergy. One wanted to know if I sold bibles. 'Sure do,' I said, 'right over there.' (Yes, under the 'Mythology' shelf marker.)

As an aside, the random thing that shocked me most was that I had more than a dozen people come in during the first week and ask for 'western' genre fiction, specifically the little paperback stories. I'd been planning and researching my shop for six months, and this entire genre had never even occurred to me. What kind of twit opens a bookshop in a rural town but doesn't sell fiction about cowboys and ranchers and cattle? Geez. I'm an idiot.

If any idle publishers are out there reading this, on behalf of a larger-than-assumed chunk of older Australian people, pretty *pretty* please, with sugar and a pineapple on top, start reprinting the dime westerns. The garage sale and Saturday fete underground can't keep up with demand.

~

Country folk look after one another. If they're of the same denomination and they cheer for the same football team.

But can we talk honestly for a moment about some of the seedier bigoted undertones of the smiling rural image that Australia likes to celebrate? Maybe we should acknowledge that those smiles, amid the wholesome simplicity of earth and gumtrees and grain stalks baking in the Queensland heat, sometimes turn startlingly hostile at the mere hint of 'other'. Difference and non-conformity seem a catalyst for whisperings and glares from the mob waiting at the school gate, or gossip around the feed store delivery truck.

It pops up in all sorts of places, and not just the 'Strayan flag-printed 'Fuck Off, We're Full' bumper stickers on utes, because Johnno heard on the pub telly that the *muzzies* are coming to take over. (Eesh.) But in supposedly more 'civilised' places too – like in the 'Ask a Local' section inevitably found in the local rag, where some journalist tries desperately to fill white space with opinions fished off the street because they can't extend the four-page 'Garden Shed – Robbed!' exposé any further, or justify yet another neighbourly whine at vandals knocking down a street sign.

People who don't fit into boxes tend to stick out like sore thumbs in small towns, and a lot of them gravitated towards my bookshop. It stood among the haberdashery and smallgoods stores in quiet protest and seemed a bit like a beacon to freaks and weirdos (and I mean freaks and weirdos only in a loving and affectionate way, of course).

A handful of adults occasionally came to listen to story-time, while others just came to sit in a comfy chair and read with a cuppa. The small sofa in my office was a popular drop-in spot, and it seems as though I heard the life story of everybody in town at one point or another. New babies, new jobs, lost jobs, deaths, illnesses, divorce and romance and STIs. Intrigue and industrial espionage, business deals and bankruptcies. My own little watermelon soap opera.

It also morphed into a go-to safe space for the sproggets of the town.

S was a familiar face at the local independent supermarket. He was gay, and he was not remotely inclined to bow to what many townsfolk perceived as common decency and conceal this fact. His flamboyant, unashamed self-expression and effervescent personality were lovely after another dreary trolley-pushing session, and I looked forward to seeing him.

But someone else didn't think so. He was eventually fired after complaints from customers … because 'reasons'. I'm sure something palatable was fabricated and stretched and used officially in place of what everybody unofficially knew to be true – that too many people had complained to management about having to suffer the service of an 'other'.

When S told me about it, he smiled sadly, shrugged a bit, let it roll off his back with a deep breath and went straight on to talking enthusiastically about whatever his next piece of news was, as though it didn't really matter.

I wanted him to be angry. To be fuming the way that I felt. But I'm not sure that he could express or even feel anger by that point. There's only so much steam that you can blow out of your ears before you run out of puff. Simple physics. When there are so many fights to be had, and not enough resources to fight them, you have to choose them carefully.

I did the only thing I could do. The last true resort left to us to impotently rail at injustice.

I wrote a letter to the local paper.

The response led to a saga of letter exchanges via the editorial column from local clergy anxious to reassure the public that it's not homophobic bigotry to hate on gay people, it's just because they're dirty sinners and, meanwhile, the church is lovingly trying to save souls.

It does tweak me a bit to imagine outraged, prudish townsfolk meeting in the dead of night, waving their torches and pitchforks while wailing at the threat that I posed to their babes: an evil bookshop that refused to sell good christian propaganda and that probably played the devil's music too! (I played a bit of Bob Marley, sometimes ... but he became a christian, so that doesn't count.)

I'm not sure what their conversations actually entailed, as obviously I wasn't invited. But not long after my letter-to-the-editor, the cafe owners two doors down shifted some of their tables, installed a few bookshelves and erected an enormous sign in their window: 'Books sold here!' Really, that sign was bigger than my sign for the whole bookshop. Turned out their cafe had become a distributor for a well-known christian publisher that shall remain nameless here. It sold only wholesome stories, such as the tale of Noah and the genocidal flood that god sent to slaughter most of humanity and a bunch of apparently deserving animals and plants along with it.

Ever the good sport, I retaliated by raising a rainbow flag in my window and starting a weekly support group for gender and sexuality diverse sprogs. It seemed the thing to do.

~

My family's world has been full of brilliant people. Too many to list and write about, so please don't hate me if I fail to mention you – writing a book is *hard*. If you know that I love you and you haven't seen your name here, I will totally make you cannelloni. Consider this page my IOU.

I met Mr Punkypiratepants (name changed to protect the awesome) before even he knew that that's who he is. Up until that point he'd been masquerading as a cute girl. As far as I saw, he liked tutus and glitter and facing everything with squealy excitement, the kind that makes you spin in circles and your head pop off. To know him is to love him. Punkably adorable. Truly, he's so frickin' beautiful that he deserves a description that you'd fall in love with too. He deserves a writer skilled enough to do that. Someone much better than me should write about him, but you get the general idea.

I had no idea how to support his transition when he told me about it. To be truthful, I didn't try too hard to understand in the beginning, either. Surely it was unreasonable for him to insist that we use male pronouns *all* the time? I'd known him so long as 'she' that this was imprinted on my mind, and I had to make *such* an effort to switch it – or so went my attitude back then. I'd never have dreamed of rejecting him because of it, but my acceptance, on my terms, was pretty crappy to start with.

It took me an embarrassingly long time to figure out that I wasn't the one being hurt by misgendering. Never one to push, he graciously suffered my fumbling attempts to come to terms with it, like my awkward comments about missing his boobage and getting to keep all his favourite girl clothes if he wasn't going to use them anymore. I think I must have run the gamut of Things Not To Say To a Transgender Man over our time together. Meanwhile, the sprogs took it in their stride.

'Mr Punkypiratepants has come out as transgender,' I told

them. 'This means that he's a man, and we use he/him/his pronouns for him.'

'Okay. What's for dinner?'

And that was that. No fanfare or discomfort. This person who we loved was still a person who we love: we just use different words now.

I'm forever grateful to Mr Punkypiratepants for letting me practise on him. It wasn't his job – it's absolutely not any transgender person's job to educate the masses as to how to treat them respectfully and lovingly – but I'm glad that he stuck in there voluntarily and showed me such patience while I figured it out. While I *still* figure it out. He has probably saved Kai from so many awkward moments with me.

Mr Punkypiratepants means way more to me than just a learning experience for my sprogs, but a side effect of being friends with him has been that he was invaluable in helping Kai to feel accepted too. In showing Kai that, while there are still wrinkles to iron out, he's still loved and lovable, still going to be okay. That, as difficult to navigate as this road is, Kai *can* reach the end of it as a successful man who has meaningful relationships, a prosperous career and an authentic experience. Mr Punkypiratepants has my undying, eternal devotion for taking on that role in Kai's life.

I feel the need to pause here and explain 'misgendering' for the sake of those reading who don't know what it is. Misgendering, in this context, is the act of either deliberately or carelessly using the wrong pronouns for a person who you know to be in transition. Nobody denies that it can be a tricky thing to switch pronouns and verbal gender markers for someone who you've known for twenty years as another name and gender – we've slipped up plenty with Kai's transition. It seems to be hardest when I'm intently focused on something else, or if I'm angry or upset and talking fast. If it happens in our family, we point it out for one another, use the correct term and keep going.

But it's vitally important that we do it. And if you slip up, I will point it out to you too.

Deliberately misgendering while talking to or discussing a transgender person is the pig-headed refusal to allow that person sovereignty over their own body. It's saying that you, in your arrogant wisdom, know better than they what gender identity they should present as, while denying them the right to define it for themselves. I tend to think that deliberately misgendering transgender people probably has a root in stereotyping – when stereotypes are used, for example, to socially shame a woman for being perceived as masculine.

Whatever the case, misgendering is a derogatory and disdainful verbal aggression. I can't even imagine how dehumanising it would be to have someone try to redefine a part of me, something that I know to be inherent. Would you insist to a woman who'd adopted a child that she isn't *technically* its mother? If so, you'd have to be a callous wanker.

Transgender people aren't delusional: they understand their own physical reality just fine. Better than we can. As I understand it, being transgender isn't a denial of that physical reality, it's a disagreement with it. It seems to me that when someone has been denied the actualisation of something for so long and is now finally able to be themselves, each 'she' in the wrong place can be another stab in the heart – a suggestion that they aren't seen as a real man, which can transport them jarringly to a place of unhappiness.

As a general rule, if you're unsure which pronouns a person would like you to use, just ask them. Truly, don't be shy. I can't speak for anybody else, obviously, but Kai says he'd be pleased that you cared enough to ask and acknowledge his right to determine for himself which pronouns he uses.

~

So it was that my sprogs were surrounded by people fighting to live true to themselves in the face of some pretty daunting odds. These awesome folk probably seemed even more exceptional to Kai and Mikey when contrasted with some of the ignorance and smallness that they also got to observe and study.

It was as if we lived in two worlds: one where everybody's aim was compassion and kindness and dignity and self-expression, where things were examined and scrutinised and gauged for improvement so that people could grow and participate in a great becoming, and another world where things were superficially endured for the sake of a connection with the rest of the town. It was like having a weird museum view into 1953, with re-enactment method actors dressed up in period costume and walking around in character to immerse you in the realities of the time, but then realising that they don't think they're in character and they're actually wondering what a digital watch is.

One time when S was chatting to me on his lunchbreak, customers came in who needed my attention, so he blew me a kiss and flitted off in his usual enthusiastic way. After he had gone, the older woman standing at the counter in front of me rolled her eyes and pulled a face in the hateful way that people do when they expect that everybody around them shares their bigotry. Angry at the thought that this woman was one of the walking reasons for the challenges that S faces, I wasn't very nice to her at all. (I gradually came to understand why so many people with principles end up poor.)

My bookshop sat in a little arcade, and in its centre was a serene fishpond that was a favourite attraction for children. Besides keeping one-eye-out for unsupervised spawn young enough to drown in the thing, I liked listening to the conversations and the exclamations of sprogget discovery.

For a period, there was a sick goldfish – you know, that terminal disease where they blow up like a balloon and their scales stick out, and then you find them floating upside-down, covered in the slime of decomposition. Most of the kids could draw on their evolutionary instincts to realise that the differently shaped member of the fish herd was probably sick. There were expressions of sadness and lessons about object permanence and mortality among the pond-side conversations, but one snippet lifted my brow: 'Look at that one, Mum! It's really round!' 'Yeah. Maybe he's pregnant?' With all solemnity. It would have been nice to think that she was including biological diversity in her kids' education about the world, but given the context the chances aren't high.

It was impossible to protect my sprogs from all the aliens walking into the bookstore. There were simply too many. For every fertile mind that would wander in, begging for literary crack to satiate the yearning for addictive knowledge, there were ten cranky old town women and goldfish mothers.

'Look, Mum! It's *Lord of the Rings* – in a BOOK!'

'Do you have a copy of *Mein Camphor*?'

'Do you stock *Twilight*?'

'Do you stock *Twilight*?'

'Do you stock that vampire book by the Mormon lady?'

Bah.

It's a wonder that I got out of it in one piece, with only a mild case of alcoholism and only a slight case of book hoarding.

That said, though, if I ignore the insipid main character, the frightening misogyny, the weak-as-piss vampires and the painfully frequent references to classical literature (a sad attempt to make the author seem learned), I credit *Twilight* with the brilliant feat of bringing masses of teenagers into the book-loving fold. Loads of them came in to say, 'I've just finished *Twilight* ... have you got anything like that?' Now that they'd been bitten by the bug, like that series was a literary gateway drug, I would gleefully show them to the fantasy section. It truly was a privilege to introduce kids to the likes of Douglas Adams and Piers Anthony, with fantastical worlds that they could build in their heads, and characters who they would fall in love with and who would belong to them, always. This sparked a new generation in town of people who always know where their towels are.

It can feel really odd to hear other people talk about books that I've loved, that I've adopted as part of my history and therefore my identity. Like listening to a stranger talk as though they know my family – don't they realise that Mr Darcy and Elizabeth Bennet are *mine*? Willingly sharing books is different, though. But I don't think that I was really meant for retail. Sometimes containing my own thoughts for the sake of customer-is-always-rightness was the hardest thing I've ever had to do. I'm not good at shushing for the sake of propriety.

~

Some of my bad mood came about because this was the time in my life that I know affectionately as the Quitting Epoch. It's distinct from the other times in my life, as it's marked by strong urges to throw things at the people I had no patience for.

I smoked like a chimney. Like a chimney that someone kept giving cigars to. My cravings were so bad that I'd begin to get agitated when my packet was starting to get low. That I would choose the places where we went out according to whether I could smoke there or not. To some extent, my smoking even dictated the people we would hang out with, because hanging out with non-smokers was a drag. Or not a drag. You know what I mean.

I had quit for a few years before the Epoch, but that had been a bit different. The farm was a million miles from anywhere, so by the time I had a craving and got in the car to go for some smokes, I could talk myself down. 'Aw, come on! You've been doing so well! If you get smokes now, you have to do this whole thing again.'

It was also easy enough to stay away from cigarettes because the farm was pretty solitary. In town, though, most of my friends smoked, and they kept dropping in for coffee and tea, all the while carrying their own little packets of sweet, sweet disgustingness. Smoking friends always say that they won't give you one, but you know that if you ask enough they will, because they secretly want their smoking buddy back to reinforce the cognitive dissonance that maintains their own destructive addiction. Devious legal junkies, one and all.

None of this was conscious, though. It's bloody hard to objectively examine the addictions that you wear while you're wearing them – but the mirror that quitting shines is fragile. Even now, I know that it would take just one weak moment and I'd be back. Every time I walk past a smokers' area, I know that I could bum one. The arsehole addiction voice in my head niggles me that I could have one and be fine. (The arsehole addiction voice in my head sounds like Kathleen Turner, just so you know how to read it.) 'Dude, you had a whole packet when you were drunk at that bamboo karaoke place in the Philippines, and that turned out fine. You can have just one now. Go ahead, you deserve it. You're under *so* much stress.'

But I don't want the headspinny shudder and ick that comes with a cig after you haven't had one for ages: I want the divine, calming, full-body peace that comes with the early-morning coffee cig of a regular smoker. I'm just not willing to be a regular smoker again to get it. Any time I'm drinking and socialising and bum one while we're chatting, I just end up feeling disgusting and remorseful, so that makes it slightly easier to resist.

Back then, I hated feeling so pathetic and out of control, and I especially hated stinking all the time and being treated like a social pariah, but I would rearrange my whole day around my cigarettes.

I've never been able to identify with those people who can have a cig out with friends and then just not have one again. They're the same as people who keep half a chocolate bar in their fridge. What the hell kind of person can only eat half a chocolate bar? Well, actually, Mikey is a weirdo like that. He buys his own stash of treats and hides them away to be eaten, one at a time, over a whole week. But Kai eats sweets like I do – he gobbles them down fast before they disappear, as though food is transient and impermanent and can be taken away from you at any moment.

I feel pretty fortunate that neither of them seems interested in a smoking habit of their own. If there was any maternal influence over that decision, along with a few others, it was probably another case of accidental parenting on my part. The old ditty about 'if you can't set a good example, at least be a horrible warning'.

They're both so much smarter than I was, about so many things. I'm amazed by how well they know themselves and how determined they are about what's right and good. This whole generation is going to shake things up. I can't wait to see it.

HOW I MET MY SON

~

The single best part of selling second-hand books is finding treasures – not just books to be treasured, but little clues about where they've come from and the people who have owned them.

Like my collection of boarding passes, each one found pressed like a bookmark between pages of new-looking books, before the start of the second chapter. I have nearly sixty of them, with all sorts of destinations, but only one that was found marking pages beyond that point: it was inside the back cover, so I can't tell how much the former owner read, or if they just tucked it in there in a hurry.

Or like the science, poetry and philosophy books with pencilled notes in the margins that tell me so much more than the book could on its own.

Opening up the front cover to find an author signature is always exciting too, but the coolest thing I've found so far would have to be the Louis L'Amour collection that I opened up and found a secret hole cut out of the yellowed pages in the rough shape of a gun. There was nothing inside it, but it was the perfect place for someone to stash one. My imagination so hopes it was a six-shooter and that the book was kept on a shelf with a bottle of whisky and a hook to hang shiny spurs from.

Not everybody shares my bookish sense of humour. I got a radio slot to advertise my store, and the marketing guy called me up to talk about designing it, as creating the ad was included in the price. I only half-jokingly asked if he could do a *War of the Worlds*-themed ad, given the huge sci-fi collection that I had, and he just ummed. 'What do you mean, Yolanda?'

'What do you mean, what do I mean? H.G. Wells? Orson Welles? Widespread panic because people thought a radio play was an actual news bulletin about aliens invading?'

'Never heard of it.'

'I think you should probably go and hand in your resignation. People who haven't heard of *War of the Worlds* aren't allowed to work in radio, I'm pretty sure. It's in the rules.'

Like a trooper, he went and googled and sent me an awesome draft of the ad as a news report, 'live' at the scene of the meteor that had crashed on my shop, but urging folk not to panic because the stock was unharmed – then tentacles appeared, and the reporter was dragged off. It was brill!

~

It's not just books that have been a family backdrop - we joke about playing *World of Warcraft* and other computer games, and most people tend to think of them as a frivolous pursuit, but they've been a huge part of our lives over the years. Having a mutual passion for something is a brilliant way to feel close to someone, and I've rarely felt closer to my kids than when we've all had our computers on the same desk, running our characters together through a dungeon (a part of the game where you work together to defeat bigger foes).

For those who don't know anything about *WoW*, it's a vividly beautiful online world that you can run around in while interacting with other players. Your character gets stronger with more experiences, and you can equip ever-fancier armour to improve your abilities. You can cast magic spells to kill monsters and generally get to be a hero. There's a very involved and complex lore, and people who love reading fantasy novels (i.e. me) just adore it.

You can be a mighty warrior, a beautiful shaman or a powerful mage, or any number of other characters that facilitate you being other than your usual mundane self. You step in and suddenly you're entrusted with world-saving tasks: the things you do matter – they can have an immediate and powerful effect on the things around you. It's not hard to understand why that appeals to people.

When Mikey was quite young, he had a mild speech impediment and struggled to make friends, and given that the social parts of school were so hard for him, he had difficulties with the reading and writing parts of it too. They tend to go hand in hand. But with games, he was forced to read so that he could progress to the next part. He was forced to cooperate, collaborate and be sociable with other kids – other kids who wouldn't tease him for not saying things properly because he wasn't talking to them, he was typing.

He really came into his own in the videogame world, and after watching his sometimes hard days in Meatspace (the not-virtual world), I loved seeing him happy. For a kid who missed out on achievements, surrounded by other academically or athletically gifted students, developing his skillset and using his ingenuity to conquer complex challenges in games gave him not only a sense of purpose, but also an important sense of accomplishment and esteem for his own abilities. Here was a place where he could be both inspired and inspiring, be passionate and committed, and participate in meaningful quests.

The drive to achieve these goals has motivated Mikey to learn programming and save for and build his own computer. He's cultivated a close-knit social circle, and watching him interact with Kai in a place where they leave the sibling bullshit behind has been great. There's no, 'Mu-um! He's got my <whatever>! Tell him to give it back!' And I can observe touching exchanges like: 'Mikey! Your health's running low. Stop running so I can give you a potion, or you'll die!' or 'I've already got a good cloak. You can have this one if you like, you need more HP.' Non-gamers probably think that sounds silly, but trust me, that's as sweet as frickin' *pie* to a gamer mother's ears.

Kai and I have a blast together. We have two teams: Gnome Rogues called SappyMcStab and StabbyMcSap, and Night Elf Priests called ConfessThis and ConfessThat.

Rogues are a sneaky, stealthy character class that can turn invisible and lie in wait for another unwitting player to come along, then they stun them, pounce on them and half-kill them before they even have a chance to retaliate. Two rogues working in partnership is a lot of fun to play in a battleground scenario.

Our priests are even better, though. As a spell-casting class and Night Elves, they can be invisible too, but only while they're standing still. They have an ability spell called 'Mind Control', which lets you take over another player's character for a few seconds. So one of our favourite pastimes is hiding on a tall bridge and Mind Controlling other players off its edge to their doom. All of their fancy armour, carefully learned spells and favourite battle strategies become useless, and they have to watch helplessly while they jump themselves off, only regaining control just as it's too late to prevent their demise. Then they have to walk all the way back from the graveyard where they respawn. Truly, that never gets old. Have you ganked someone with your sprogget today?

If those benefits still aren't enough to convince you that you should be gaming with your kids, I'll tell you about how neat it feels to sit and bask in teenage reverence while your sprog regales their friends with stories of your guild's epic Heroic Deathwing conquest, and they turn and regard your wise sage self with widened eyes and a new perspective of awe. Out here, I'm a podgy middle-aged student who could avatar as every mother-next-door, but in there, I'm also awesome. *We're* awesome.

When we aren't on the computer, we keep ourselves amused by playing altruistic pranks, our version of positive Meatspace trolling. Our all-time favourite prank to play, up until the highways switched to the automated tag system, was to pay the toll of the car behind us when we went through a booth. The sprogs would laugh hysterically as they watched, in the rear window as we drove off, the other driver arguing with the attendant, trying to tell them that they didn't know us. Now that I think about it, it probably drove the attendants nuts. Sorry, attendants!

Another favourite of ours is good-will noticeboard additions.

You know the adverts that people use to sell their bikes and puppies and things with the tear-off strips of phone numbers that end up waving all over the place? We write 'Free Compliments and Encouragement – Please take what you need.' And instead of phone numbers, the tabs say things like 'You're awesome!' and 'You can do it – we believe in you!' etc. We put them up, then run away like big giggling dorks.

We've never been much into organised activities, and while we tried the usual sports and music lesson-type extracurricular stuff, none of us are very good at sticking to things. But this stuff, making our own fun? We've got that down pat.

~

Mum: Sprogget … I'm hungry.

      Kai: So make something to eat then, silly.

Mum: I had too much wine already. It's not safe. I ate the chocolate, but it just made my wine taste funny.

      Kai: I'm in bed. Can't Mikey do it?

Mum: His Facebook is off, and I didn't finish installing a sense of guilt and obligation in him yet, so he's much harder to persuade. I bought you one of those custard danishes that you like. Will you make it for me?

      Kai: You bought me a danish and you want me to cook it for you?

Mum: You can have some too.

Kai: I'm not hungry. I'll put it in the oven.

Mum: And when it's done can you take it out again?

Kai: You want me to bring it to you as well?

Mum: I don't want to put you to any trouble.

Kai: ...

7

Letters from the Brink

I think, therefore I am. So, if conscious thought defines something's existence, if I don't think about it, is it really happening at all?

TOWARDS THE END of his senior year, I got a call from Kai's school, asking me to come in to speak with him and the guidance counsellor. He'd revealed that he had been cutting himself and having suicidal ideations (thoughts of killing himself). I don't think I've ever been so afraid.

The noise in my ears drowned out the stranger in front of me, who was trying to tell me about my sprogget's pain. Did she think

I didn't know? I'd helplessly watched it grow for years. I'd stood on what I realised was the other side of the wall that he'd built around himself, knocking my knuckles bloody trying to get him to open it. He sat, curled in on himself, like he had a great, invisible weight bearing down on him and no hope of ever being free of it. He was within arm's reach, but arm's reach was a vast introspective chasm.

Why is 'Mum' paradoxically the person who you know loves you most in all the world, but also the person who you think least likely to understand what you're going through? It's a label that means the best cuddles, but automatically precludes access to those deep, aching pains in your heart.

We've debated how to write about this dark period for months, Kai and I. There's still so much stigma that goes along with mental health issues, and it's not like Kai doesn't have enough stigma to face already. But it's important to both of us that the people out there going through the same thing (or similar things) understand that they are not alone. The only thing that's ever going to really shake that stigma is people refusing to wear it. This is us, refusing to wear it.

~

It's not fair to ask Kai to bare the inside of some of the darkest corners of his head to the whole world and stand out there all alone, so I will open mine first. (You might understand our reaction better if you know some of the history too.)

In February 1988, my father took his own life. My mother moved me and my siblings to Australia in January 1989 in search of a fresh start, but we were still pretty scarred, and it's not so easy to mop up messes like that. I've long since been diagnosed with PTSD, while reflection has given me more insight not just into myself, but also into the people and events surrounding me.

The shadows followed us even when we settled on the Central Coast in New South Wales, surrounded by beautiful beaches and pristine bushland. In comparison to the grey and rainy tones of the little UK town that I'd grown up in so far, it was paradise, but the grief still manifested itself – in all sorts of odd and disconnected ways. Mum and I struggled to maintain a relationship, and I found myself flitting between youth refuges, foster homes and street havens, each of which come with their own associated problems. The setting really just made it a prettier, and warmer, place to fall apart.

I know that it's painful for my mum to remember too – maybe it'll give us some resolution, Mum? Maybe, but even if it doesn't, this is my story. Parts of it are ugly and undignified, but I'm not ashamed of it. It's okay to not seem so shiny all the time. It's alright to be vulnerable and say that things aren't okay. Rugs are for warming your feet, not hiding shit from the neighbours, because the stink is still there when you do and eventually it all spills out anyways.

I think that so much of the destructive power of mental health issues comes about because people spend so much energy trying to hide them. That concealing them and trying to appear neurotypical becomes more important than dealing with the problems themselves.

In the interests of disclosure: Hi, my name is Yolanda and I suffer from PTSD, anxiety and depression. I am a survivor of rape, and I have experienced homelessness and dependency. I've used a number of destructive escapist habits over the years – including running away and pharmaceutical-grade denial, heavy smoking, drinking too much and too often, engaging in some pretty unhealthy sexual relationships as well as a food addiction.

Anxiety and depression at the same time are a peculiar combo to have – to be simultaneously apathetic and frantic is no small feat. The anxiety part is like having another person following you around, constantly shaking and prodding you, second-guessing everything you do and reminding you of everything that is wrong, all the time. The depression part is yet another person following that guy and answering them with 'Dude, shut up.' Sometimes you can only cope with that constant bickering in your head by sticking your fingers in your ears and blocking everything out entirely.

To calm myself down at times, I name Henry VIII's wives in order in my head. If I'm very anxious, I name his children too. If things get really dire, I list mistresses and scandals. It works pretty well. I did try a Zen garden for a while – it's just a box of sand, three pebbles and a tiny rake so that you can find peace by endlessly trying to rake the sand into a symmetrical pattern around the rocks. Only, each time that you rake, the prongs intrude on the beautifully straight lines of the raking before – so you become trapped and ever-more anxious in an eternal battle of asymmetry until you break and hide it in a draw, only to find it months later when it spills sand all through your stationery and makes it gross.

~

Hindsight is spring water, but at the time, it was a muddy period of early teenage chaos, where so much energy is spent just reacting to things, there isn't any left over for really living. What I now understand to be anxiety was wildly confusing back then. This was before the masses had easy access to the internet along with all the information and social support that we now take for granted. I was broken, and for all I knew, I was the only person in the world who felt this way.

Running away was my escape drug of choice. I discovered that when things were shitty and I couldn't deal with them, it was much easier to just not be there. Overwhelming emotions? No problem, just relocate. The kid in the bedroom next door at the youth refuge says she's going to stab you in your sleep? Not a big deal, just go out the window. Sitting in the cold on a deserted train station is preferable to having to make polite conversation with some creepy sleazebag back there where it was warm. There were so many reasons to not be where I was, wherever it was.

The triggers for this were many and varied – some of them you might consider more justifiable as reasons than others, but at the time they all seemed equally huge. A douchebag youth worker feeling you up is a pretty good reason to go away, whereas leaving because you're pissed off that someone stole your *Cooleyhighharmony* album, not so much. (Okay, owning up to having a Boyz II Men CD should stay under the rug, you're right.) When you're fourteen, everything gets an equal allotment of dramatic reaction, and when a voice in your mind is constantly screaming 'The sky is falling! The sky is falling!' it can be hard to tell the actual issues from the non.

The problem with running away and not giving adult-brained due consideration to consequences is that you sometimes end up in places that are worse than when you started. I have a couple of pictures of myself at that age, and I want to reach into them and tell that girl to stop – that things will be alright. She looks so small and vulnerable that it kills me to think of the dangerous places that she found herself in.

I remember feeling so frightened, sometimes – but then other times, when I should have been scared, I totally underestimated the danger and overestimated myself. Teenage immortality complex mixed with risky situations equals badness.

I learned very quickly that some men would be the first to take advantage of that vulnerability and, shortly after that, determined that the men in positions of power or authority were the most likely to abuse it. It became a perilous seesaw: I was leery of men and, at the same time, enthralled by the superficial and temporary acceptance and love that indiscriminate promiscuity with them supplied. I, who felt powerless and insignificant most of the time, had an illusion of control over something because I could provoke certain reactions. Don't get me wrong, I'm very sex-positive and consider a hearty enjoyment of sex to be a healthy thing, but these relationships were not healthy. They weren't a robust and lusty sexual expression by consenting equals: they were cries for affection, protection and stability that were answered mostly by those all too happy to exploit me.

It was a contradiction to be told that I was beautiful and special and valuable at the same time as being demeaned and discarded. It has taken a long, long time to mend the devastation that this conflict wrought on my self-esteem.

~

Youth refuges can be temporary or long-term group homes for troubled sprogs, some of them better places than others. I can't speak for how they are now, but they used to have a rotating roster of youth workers who stayed on premises, and some of these were better than others too. There are all types of facilities – some were dumps covered in graffiti and with walls more hole than plaster, where you were given a toothbrush, handed a sheet and pointed towards a dirty foam mattress in a shared room. Others were just your average suburban quarter-acre brick facade that could have been anybody's home.

One that I stayed in for a while was funded by a wealthy philanthropist and looked like one of those McMansions that you only see on American TV shows, with panelled wood and lovely paintings everywhere. I got a room with a cushioned window seat and a beautiful, high ceiling with exposed beams. It was surreal. It was a home where people had taken the time to paint wee flowers on the ornamental ceramic window catches and carved scrollwork in the doorjambs. I'd never seen anything like it. You figure out pretty quickly that it's just landscaping, though. Same shit, different wallpaper.

However beautiful or stark, the atmosphere in all the homes was volatile and depended entirely on the mix of kids who were currently staying there. Arriving at a new place was always a dicey affair. Each dynamic had to readjust to accommodate someone unknown, and it could take a while before the pecking order became established. Chests were beaten, bravado was strutted and street cred was sized up, like a goat herd figuring out who is to lead and who is to follow.

A melting pot with varying levels and types of dysfunction and trauma could be an interesting recipe that led to interesting times, but mostly there was just pain. Some sprogs were unwanted and unloved – some just thought they were because, for whatever reason, they couldn't maintain familial connections and cultivated some confused and frustrated parents. Thing is, the perception of a thing can be enough to provoke the same reaction as the thing itself, so a sprog who feels unwanted manifests the same legitimate crappy brokenness.

Many kids face trauma and don't end up in youth refuges or on the streets. I've always wondered what it is that means that some sprogs are resilient and weather difficulties while others fall to pieces, and I've come to the tentative conclusion that mental illness plays a substantial part. The sprogs who I shared experiences with displayed decisive manifestations of mental illness: self-harm, suicidal ideations and attempts, hyper-aggression, substance abuse, some messed-up sexual behaviours. You could pretty much play symptom bingo during any given week. (I should add a disclaimer that these are my totally amateur observations and nothing more.)

Still others who might have started out as mere 'troubled' kids find themselves suddenly with a full-blown case of 'delinquency' thanks to the traumas inflicted by a flawed system that's supposed to be there to protect them.

I was jostled around from place to place. Sometimes this was my doing, sometimes not, but it meant that staying in one school long enough to make actual real friends was a fantasy. Friendships with the other refuge kids didn't count because they were just half-people too. In those relationships there was a juxtaposition of closeness in the way that shared intense experiences form a bond, but also distance because there were so many walls up and so much defensive posturing that you never really got to know each other. It's too much work surviving yourself in that situation, without having to feel for someone else's hurts as well.

Watching other sprogs at school, with packed lunches and the normalcy of parents to pick them up afterwards, was difficult. There were a thousand ways to reinforce the 'other' of me. Like being called into the teacher's office on the first day at a new school to be lectured on how she's 'just gotten this class in line' and how she 'won't tolerate shit from some refuge kid disrupting the peace'. The irony is, I'd never have dreamed of being deliberately disruptive until she gave my fourteen-year-old self a reason to feel belittled and humiliated and cook up a high school-sized grudge that finished with a puddle of glue on her car seat. Sorry, lady.

Admonishment for crimes that I was assumed to be planning or to have committed became a pretty common feature. (Which is probably why my hackles rose so easily when I could see the same thing happening to Kai at high school.) I got so sensitised to it that I built up quite a repertoire of sideways vengeance – I had a strangely developed sense of justice by that point.

But most of my angst was turned inwards. At the height of summer when I get a decent tan, the scar lines on my arms and legs become more distinct, an ancient reminder of desperately trying to feel something, anything, other than what I was feeling. I couldn't influence or control most things, but that was just mine. My body was the only thing that only I owned, and it felt good to have tangible proof.

~

In between stints in group homes and my Houdini acts, I spent some time in foster care. Like the refuges, these varied wildly, and you never knew what you were going to get until you arrived. Even in the best ones, it's uniquely dehumanising to be dragged to church so that your foster family can show off this week's project and have everybody tell you how lucky you are to be taken in by such great people.

But really, if that's your only complaint about them, you're probably doing okay. There are definitely worse ways to have it. Let's just skip talking about foster care. There's plenty wrong with it, but it feels ungrateful to say much else except 'thank you' and shut up.

The other option was sleeping in the open. Not so great, but there were times when it was the better one. It came with its own special hazards. The kind of cold that you feel in your bones. Being damp and not being able to get dry, even if you did find somewhere inside to be for a while. Then, of course, there's the people. The people can be the scariest part of anything.

A certain type of clothing donation bin can be a good place to sleep if you're small enough to squeeze through the big flap. Unless the bin's empty, in which case you're gonna be cold and it's going to be hard to get out. But you don't want it to be too full, either, otherwise you have to crawl out backwards and empty it a bit so that there's room for you. You probably shouldn't tell anybody else that that's where you like to sleep, either, coz they'll take it.

I tried to get in my favourite one, once, but the flap wouldn't open. I pushed on it some, but it only budged a little. I pushed a bit harder.

'Fuck off.'

'Who's that?'

'Nobody. Fuck off. This one's mine.'

I went to another one but got woken up by screeching tyres, car doors slamming and a couple having the worst row I've ever seen. I was too scared to look, but they didn't notice me.

That was a fairly typical night. There were other places to sleep, though. Sometimes you meet people and when they find out, they take you home – like a stray puppy. I think the altruism tickles some folk, but realities are more difficult than a shower and a meal. There was usually some price to pay for it too. It wasn't only once that I was okay with snuggling someone because his (or her) bed was warm and soft and outside was cold and wet. It was some *Sweet Charity* crap, for sure.

'C'mon, baby, give me your number.'

'What for?'

'I just want to make sure you get home alright.'

'You don't know my name or where I live. What exactly is it that you propose to do if I don't make it home?' Or, as I would have said it back then, 'Fuck off, wanker.'

I was a bit surprised when one woman left her three small kids with me so that she could go out. 'I'm just gonna drop into the club to see if I won the raffle, won't be long. You don't mind, do you?' She'd known me two hours and all she knew about me was that I needed somewhere to go. *I* know that I'd never have hurt them, but *she* didn't – she's lucky that she didn't come home and find them duct-taped to the wall.

Another woman fed me in return for me going in to the doctor and telling him that I couldn't sleep and that I was hearing voices because I'd been awake too long, so that she could have a prescription. I must have got the wrong thing, though, because she was cranky when I came out. 'These aren't what I want! These are psych drugs!' And she just tore up the packet and left while I ate my burger and watched her go. Looking back at it now, that GP was pretty irresponsible with his prescription pad after a five-minute consult.

You could shrug most of that stuff away with humour, with 'people are just weird', but not the scary ones. Like the time I was hitching and a driver bought me dinner. Something had a funny petrol aftertaste, and I started feeling strange as we hung out for a bit smoking, then walked back to his truck. I figured it out just as he was pulling out of the truck stop, so I opened the door and jumped (fell), then spent the rest of the night drinking awful coffee, sitting on the hard picnic bench seats and trying to shake off a seriously fuzzy head that had me gazing at my fingers and marvelling at how weirdly shaped they were and how oddly they seemed to sit in the space around me.

I eventually found a place in a long-term group home that facilitated me finishing Year Nine through an accelerated distance education program. It wasn't all smooth sailing – the girls there were the interesting cases who struggled everywhere else, so it could be intense at times, but overall it was the most stable I'd been in ages.

Mum visited and, while things were still raw, I think she was relieved to have a substantial timeout where she wouldn't get calls from the police at 3am. I was pretty hard work.

I hitched north with one of the other regular girls there once because she wanted to see her boyfriend. While we were away I ended up with a tattoo, alcohol poisoning, a cracked rib and a fat lip. That was a typical weekend. The atypical weekend was when her boyfriend came down to see her and held the poor social worker at knife-point so that she could get out. That was less fun.

This whole era is muddled for me, so my telling of it may not be especially linear or logically arranged – sorry about that. I think that when it comes to memories, the order that you remember them in has more to do with the size of them in your head than the place of them in time.

~

One of the memories that stands out in my head, in among all the other lunacy, was a suicide attempt that I made with a bottle of pills. I don't remember the specifics of the 'why' part – it's all a Kandinsky-esque jumble of shapes and colours. Pain and anger and shame and loneliness and drowning in it all. I couldn't make my heart slow down or my head stop racing, and I just wanted it to stop. Not existing at all seemed like the most beautiful, peaceful thing.

I was taken to hospital and had my stomach pumped – which really is as awful as it sounds, but still, probably a better option than having no liver, it's true. I was very lucky: one of the largely unseen and unmentioned consequences of suicide attempts is only managing to kill parts of yourself, so that you have to live with, or not live with, organ damage afterwards.

One nurse was particularly stern and harsh while they were pushing fluids down the tube in my throat. She had the detached matronly brusqueness down pat and wore a firmly etched frown. I felt as though I was suffocating and entirely alone, with ick coming up everywhere. If I looked half as wretched as I felt, it must have been a pitiful sight.

As I peered out of my bubble of puke and misery, her face just seemed to break, and she squeezed my hand. 'Aww, honey. You'll be okay. The only way to go from here is up.' And she blinked away a tear of her own. It wouldn't have occurred to me at the time to think that it must have been a bloody awful thing for her to have to do. Just a taste of kindness at the wrong moment had me sobbing and spluttering up snot as well as puke. It was seriously yuck.

I managed to cough the tube up before they were finished, and they made to put it back in for the liquid charcoal flush at the end. I couldn't bear the thought of a second act, so they gave me a compromise: no more tube if I swallowed three cups of it on my own. That stupid cinnamon challenge that went around a little while ago has nothing on liquid charcoal – it was like drinking an ashtray that had been left out in the rain. They didn't think I'd make it through the last cup. If only I could have been so determined about achieving goals that actually mattered.

Mum got called to come and pick me up when they were done with me in the hospital. I can only imagine what that did to her, but all I heard was her tearful admonishment of 'Why do you keep doing this to me?' And I got to twist and cook up a resentful memory of yet another time when her focus seemed to be on how she felt and how my actions appeared, rather than me feeling cared for and loved. When it was my turn, I couldn't have said the right thing to Kai for all the tea chests in Ikea, but I've been angry at my mum for not being able to for years.

All these years later, sometimes these memories are so small that

I can push them aside and smother them with beautiful things until they almost don't exist anymore, and there have been times when I've managed to convince myself that it was just a bad dream, that it didn't really happen, but that doesn't work all the time. Sometimes it grows like James' peach and snaps the tree.

What seems like a huge and significant part of my life was actually only a few years. At fifteen, I fell pregnant with Kai, and it was like the whole world suddenly righted itself. The majority of the time, a teenager with no resources and no prospects falling pregnant is not such a great thing, but I'm pretty sure that Kai saved my life. Sure, it was still relatively tumultuous and chaotic, but now there was a calm in the storm and the promise of a beautiful safe harbour of family for both of us one day. His lovely porcelain doll features and the precious tiny noises that he would make as he fed were a potent balm, and that's really when I started to see a possible future that was something to look forward to. I hushed a thousand inner voices to make things right for him.

The problem with telling these stories is that, although they're things I've lived through, they aren't representative of me and they haven't been for a very long time. Telling these stories, you fret that you become a two-dimensional representation of an issue or a cause in people's minds, rather than a whole person who has lived a hundred other lives since then.

After Kai and Mikey were born, I struggled financially, sure, but it was nothing like my earlier years. We didn't have much, but we were happy. We had our dragons and our pillow forts, and things were good. The world righted itself. So it feels weird to own this history because it's so disconnected from now.

~

Cut to nearly middle age, skip past the farming epoch, the bookshop era and a bunch of years in between, and we seem like every regular suburban family – to look at me, you'd never have guessed any of these things about me if I hadn't told you. It took a long time, but I finally felt normal. Average. Mediocre, even. It was great.

But I blinked, and suddenly my youth was gone and I was watching it replay in a sequelled version 2.0. It was so long ago, I'd consigned those memories to the distant past and nearly managed to convince myself that I was a different person, that it didn't have any bearing on the growed-up I was now, yet it was right there again, all caught up with me too. How could I not have noticed that now we had matching scars? Quite literally – he had cut in exactly the same way in exactly the same place as I used to, and the overwhelming misery I saw in his eyes made them just like a mirror.

I had sat in exactly the same chair, and though I had been in such a similar emotional place (minus the transgender experience, of course), I still had absolutely no idea how to help him or what to say. So I said and did all the wrong things. I don't actually know what I said, but I know that it was probably wrong. I think I just fell to pieces a little.

How the hell did I not notice that? He looks so small. Who

even is this woman? What's she saying? Damn, I didn't catch that. Something about some policy ... action plan? What? God, my poor sprogget. How did this happen? His shoelaces are tangled. He told me he needed new shoes last week, and I forgot. Fuck. I am the worst mother ever. A razor? What razor? I just want to hug him. Shit. I need a hug. Are you okay, sprogget? What's next? No, I don't care what you report, how do we fix him? I don't know what to do. I don't know what to do. Stop smiling pityingly at him like he's asked for jellybeans and you've only got black ones left, that's not comforting. Why won't he look at me? Your mascara is all goopy, lady. Did I lock the car? Fuck the car, your sprog needs you. My sprog needs someone who knows what they're doing. Shall I take him to the doctor? Okay, I'll take him to the doctor. Is it a doctor who we're supposed to see? Is there even a procedure for this? No, I don't care about his classes this afternoon, just write him a note or something. Are you okay, sprogget? Gawd, no I don't want to stop by the front desk and get him a pass, I don't give a shit about passes. Am I saying the wrong things? How can there be right things? What words are there that mean 'Please don't die!'? I can't breathe. Fuck. Where's Guy? What do you need from me, sprogget? Let's go to the GP, k? Okay, driving. I can do that. Has he eaten? I might have some mints in the glovebox. No, they're probably icky by now. How did this happen? Dad, me, him ... Fuck. Are we just broken? Am I speeding? No, I'm going too slow. It's an eighty zone here, right? Do I need money for the doctor? No, they bulk bill. You already know that. Will he need an appointment? I'll call. No, don't call, just drive. Figure it out when you get there. Figure what out? Nothing is figured out. Crap. He looks like he's been crying for a month. Are you okay, sprogget? We'll be there soon. Stop asking if he's okay. He's obviously not okay. I'm not okay. Nothing is okay. It can be okay. Chill out, you're panicking him. Just breathe. Be reassuring. Why are you not more reassuring??? Things are fine and this is no big deal, you can totally recover from this, kiddo. No big deal? Are you kidding? That's not reassuring, that's dismissive. Well I don't fucking know. I love you. Yeah, that's better. I love you. We're gonna be okay. Are you okay? Do you want me to come in with you? Okay, I'll wait here. Take as long as you need to. No, I don't have my Medicare card, lady. We've been coming here for three years, can't you look on the file? No, I'm not driving home to get it. Here, have some money. Shit. Have I got money? Oh, okay, here's my Medicare card. I do have it. What's he doing in there? Has he been in too long? Stop it, it's only been four minutes. No! Don't touch those magazines. Eww. How did this happen? Stop shaking, hands. Don't cry. Don't cry. Don't cry. He's out already? It's only been six minutes! Go to the hospital? How does this douchebag know that he needs to be in a psych ward after six minutes of conversation? Shit. Are you okay, sprogget? Calm down, you're not helping him. Cry later. You'll make him feel worse. You're just making him feel worse. Two weeks? He'll miss his exams. Fuck his exams. Fix the sprogget now, figure out exams later. Hospital. Suicide watch. Mental health record. He'll never be able to fill out an employment form without being reminded of today. If they write it down, then it's really real. Shit. What do I do? How can he not know how much I love him? He hates needles. They might give him needles and he'll be frightened. He might have died! Are you okay, sprogget? I can't even ... Fuck. I can't. Breathe. Breathe.

I would have fought the whole world to protect him, but I had no idea how to protect him from himself on my own. I knew that it was something that needed real help, if not the hospital, so I took him to a local clinical psychologist who spent the afternoon with him, and we left with a plan. We got home and did the only successful mental health treatment that I knew – we built a pillow and doona fort and shut the world out for a bit, hibernating like chocolate-biscuit-eating bears and watching episodes of *Buffy the Vampire Slayer*.

Things were going to be okay. Not today, but eventually.

I want to say that we had a reassuring movie talk and then hugged and walked into the sunset, happily ever after, but life just isn't like that. The reality of depression and anxiety doesn't look anything like that picture at all. It's not being adorable in oversized pyjamas with mussed-up hair and binging on chocolate until the feelings go away, or a crowd of upbeat friends dragging you out for a night on the town so you cheer up. It's yelling and saying the wrong things and crying snottily through fear and pain at the thought of losing things, or facing things. It's not being able to cook up the motivation to care for yourself properly, so sometimes you realise that it's Thursday and remember that you haven't had a shower since Sunday night, when you started that Terry Brooks saga because it's way more important to find out where the Sword of Shannara is than to not stink. Even though you've already read that series and you already know how it bloody ends.

It's procrastinating and sabotaging yourself, throwing away amazing opportunities because you can't even picture yourself having achieved them. The closer you get to finishing things, the more paralysed you are by the thought of doing what needs to be done to finish them. It's like that thing where you can move halfway to a point, then halfway again, then halfway over again and again, until you're micrometres away from your goal, but every time you move, you're moving less and never getting there.

Other people tearing their hair out in frustration and despair because they can't believe that you just didn't show up to that job interview or make that one important phone call or pay that bill. It's pushing away the people that you've somehow persuaded to love you, because you're afraid that they'll see what a doofus you really are and stop – relationships that are worth so much to you, for all the effort of swimming against your intuitive currents to cultivate them in the first place.

You neglect yourself and the space and people around you because cleaning up a mess afterwards seems easier than not making it in the first place. You somehow find the energy to freak out about the most absurdly insignificant details, but can't find the strength to do the easiest thing that really matters.

You are cursed with the perfect clarity of understanding just how much sense this doesn't make. As though you're looking at yourself from outside like some macabre spectacle, watching yourself make mistakes and being an utter twit. Cursed as well to watch your sprogget doing exactly the same thing and just as unable to help him as yourself. It's not glamorous or romantic at all, and it doesn't make for a very exciting memoir.

We slowly picked up the pieces of Kai together, and focused on hope and planning for the future. We talk about it pragmatically, because shame doesn't belong attached to illness, and that's how we will continue to confront it – for both of us.

~

That's us covered, but it's easy to forget that there are other lost sproggets who are trying to fight their way through the same bullshit bureaucracy and upheaval.

For a very long time I've wanted to be a foster parent myself. My huge house feels ever emptier as the sprogs grow older and are here less and less, and I've always felt that there was room in our lives to give some of the care that I received back. Only, you know, without the indoctrination, humiliation and abuse.

I think maybe I'd have something to offer teenage foster sproggets going through similar things to my experience.

Guy and I did spend about eighteen months going through the application process. We went to all the training and did all the paperwork. We even spent some time modifying the house to be sprogget-friendly and set up a multi-age children's room to be ready. But as the jumping through hoops part dragged on and on without seeming to get anywhere – and then things didn't seem to be improving for Kai – we got disheartened and decided that it wasn't the right time for us.

Though, I'd love to revisit that idea again one day when I'm on my own and the sprogs have abandoned me to wither away in my old age, cold and alone because they won't give me grandchildren to love or visit me enough. (Text-based manipulation is hard, so you'll just have to imagine the implied pathetic sniff and the not-subtle wobble of my lower lip as you read.)

~

It seems to me that mental health is a cross-generational problem – we can examine our ancestors and make predictions about our progeny. There's some really interesting behavioural science studies out there on inherited trauma effects, and if I didn't harbour a secret worry that if we were ever examined too closely, we'd probably end up behind plate glass somewhere, I'd sign my family up as subjects.

I'm a little fuzzy on the details, but the story of my opa and oma should be an epic movie in its own right. From family stories, I understand that during the war they lived in Dordrecht, Holland, and Opa got involved with the Dutch Resistance, a largely passive movement of squirrelling away at-risk people to keep them safe from the invading Germans. Entirely Anne Frankish, if that's the mental picture that this conjured up.

In an effort to uncover where he was hiding, the Nazis took Oma and her two daughters (my aunts – Dad wasn't born until after the war) into custody. The girls were eventually let go and sent to live with farming family in the north, but Oma had it pretty rough. She was tortured. I'm not sure if it was for information or not, because by all accounts she didn't know where Opa was either.

They never did catch him, but the country suffered a dreadful winter of famine. Nobody had any food, and the Nazis consumed resources like locusts. People ate tulip bulbs to stay alive before they were freed that spring.

I can only imagine what she suffered. It's hardly a story you tell to your children over a plate of poffertjes and poedersuiker, so I don't think anybody knows the full extent of it, but she had violent nightmares for many years that would wake the whole house.

There were so many families left with long-term scars, and their story certainly isn't unique, but no less awful for it.

David Helfgott came to town for a concert in 2008, and I dressed everybody up and dragged them along with me. It wasn't very often that I could get Guy in a suit, but Mikey has always loved them. I'm pretty sure that Kai wore jeans and sneakers. We sat not six metres away from David as he played, just close enough to hear him murmuring to himself things like: 'Not too fast now, David ...' and 'We've got to be careful here, don't we?' and even an 'Ooops!' as he apparently made a mistake that only he would have noticed.

He's taken quite a bashing from music critics who scoff at him being called a genius by ignorant neophytes in love with a marketing campaign. And I guess there's an element of that. The movie about his life is sensationalistic, and I understand how stories can be twisted and personalities exaggerated for the sake of drama.

His playing is creative to say the least. Anybody looking for a literal and true rendition of sheet music might be disappointed. But there is a peace in it – a joy. Like an impressionist painting: some would find the cloudy picture nowhere near what the original model looks like, but it's beautiful as an interpretation nonetheless.

My father was of David's generation. The product of a group of people clawing to reclaim their humanity after World War II. How do a people recover from that? Can they pick up, shake themselves off and go on with things? Or does it, as I suspect, trickle down through the generations and manifest as things like David's troubled mind and my father's life cut too short?

Kai

It's hard to look backwards and reflect on my depression, especially given the context. I was lonely, sure, but I had a small circle of friends and supportive parents, and I was doing well in school. I didn't understand why I felt so down and anxious all the time.

I think that a big part of the bother of depression is guilt for feeling depressed because you don't think your depression is justified. Depression doesn't always correlate with external events. You can look around and see people with much bigger problems, so you feel selfish for spending so much time looking inwards. This is compounded in high school because the disciplinary setting isn't geared to cope with students who aren't resilient enough to weather it. Compliance with seemingly arbitrary rules, many set up to reinforce the control of the overseers rather than to serve any practical development or educational purpose, fertilises the seeds of frustration.

Towards the end of Year Twelve, so many things came to a head. I had been struggling with English and managed to conceal it until it mattered, during my end-of-year assessments. My gender dysphoria gnawed persistently at the back of my consciousness, and the general emotional chaos of being eighteen caught up with me.

It was too much, and I found myself sitting, staring out, watching a whirlwind of panicked adults freaking out after I confessed to my student counsellor that I'd had suicidal thoughts. (I've skipped a description here of any actual attempt. Those who've been there know exactly what I'm talking about, but no description would be adequate to portray it for someone who hasn't.)

The counsellor tried her best to be comforting and reassuring in her reaction, but she was practically slowly backing away towards the phone at the same time, so it pretty much spoiled the effect. The phone might as well have been a doomsday button, because she pressed it and the world exploded.

Now we needed to have 'meetings'. There had been a suicide that succeeded by a student from our school the previous year, and I think their reaction was concentrated and condensed by the myriad policies and debriefing procedural memos that must fly about after something like that. And by the urgency that being touched by an event can muster, of course. I'm sure they cover mental health issues in teaching degrees, somewhere, but it's a bit different when it's not in the abstract.

Mum was called. Her history meant that we were both desperately trying not to lay guilt on the other. Me, hyper-aware that she would be reliving her dad not living through this, and her, hyper-aware that I was aware and trying not to let that overtake her looking after me. She was trying so obviously hard not to freak out that it was really freaky. You know how you try so hard not to cry when you're upset, but that just makes you cry harder? That.

I don't remember much of what went on with that meeting. Mostly a bunch of adultish words that didn't seem to mean anything to me at the time. I just wanted to be anywhere but there. Truly, even English. Even an English exam. Even NAPLAN.

We got out of there and into the car – neither of us knew what to say to each other. Mum tried, but I think maybe I broke her. She kept talking round and round in circles like one of those pull-string dolls when the string gets broken. If it hadn't been such a messed-up day, it would have been funny.

She took me to the doctor's, and I went in by myself. It didn't seem to last long – I think I only said a handful of words, and he solemnly handed me a referral. What he suggested sounded really scary. I didn't want to go to hospital, and Mum seemed relieved. She didn't want me to go either. So she said she would find some other help, and she squeezed my hand as we got in the car. I remember it was pretty awkward – things are still a bit fuzzy. I think freaky days make for fuzzy memories.

She took me to a shrink who turned out to be really cool. She spent ages with me, and it was nice to have someone who seemed to know what was going on with me who could reassure me that it wasn't the end of the world and that I could recover. She had great hair, but she was still kinda professional and adultish.

It wasn't until we got home that I started feeling like things would get better. Till then I mostly just wanted to disappear and shut the world out hard enough that it went away forever.

Mum knew that telling me to cheer up wasn't going to cut it, and she never said that, but I could see the unspoken frustration anyway – even someone who knows that it's not something you can snap out of – or even that anything external has any power over it at all – bangs their head against the futility of it.

We watched *Buffy* and *Angel* episodes from season beginning to end (because it's a requirement that you watch them in order and series to appreciate them properly), and it was great to pretend that the rest of the world didn't exist for a while. That heroes really did conquer the biggest baddest, and that love set to crappy soundtracks and goofy subplots really does come true.

I spent a couple of weeks away from school, which was hard right in the middle of Year Twelve final exams, but I'm glad that I didn't miss them entirely, languishing in some shitty *Girl, Interrupted* set. It would have meant a lot more catching up and recovery.

The hardest part was watching everybody around me walking on eggshells or handling me like a grenade with its pin taken out. I just wanted them to be normal. I just wanted everything to be normal. Nothing had been normal before, but maybe we could give normal a shot? It was like an afternoon special, but only half the players had been given a script.

It was crap. Really crap. But not as crap as it would have been if people had let go of the lifeline when I needed them to hang on for me, so I guess I could deal.

I still struggle with depression and spend a lot of time in my batcave (aka bedroom, which by the way you still haven't tidied ~ Mum) [Yes I have! Get the feck out of my story, Mum! You have a whole rest of the book] playing *Grand Theft Auto*, but I have a bunch of coping strategies and a buttload of supportive family and friends, so the future is looking relatively bright.

I want to say that if there's anybody out there in the same position, please don't give up. Don't give in. I won't lie – you'll be battered and bruised a lot when you come out the other side, but hang in there. For five more minutes. Then for five minutes more. Five turns into thirty, and even in that short amount of time, things can look different.

Okay, I'm done now. I'll hand the manuscript back to Mum. I think she's gonna write a letter to Grandma, and I've gotta see this.

To my mum,

We don't speak often, and when we do, it's not really deeply, is it?

I call interstate to ask you how Mick's going, and you say he's fine. You ask how the kids are going, and I say they're fine. And then you finish it off with 'I don't think I've got any more news.'

I want to tell you about the things that I'm doing, or thinking about, or feeling. I want to tell you that today I read a book that had me crying on the bus because it was so touchingly beautiful — it described someone's sprogget inconsolably heartbroken because they left their blankie on a train. Or that I've been taking pictures of these fascinating beetles that I keep finding on campus, which look like tiny painted warshields. My world is beautiful, and I wish I could share it with you that way.

I want to show you the view from my pool at night when I float on my back (surely the best part of being fat is the buoyancy?) and look at the stars, and I wonder if you do that in yours? I've never seen you just float in the pool — you always seem to start right away on laps.

I want to tell you when things aren't alright, too — and so often they're not, lately. Sometimes it feels like I'm drowning in not-alright, and I wish that there were someone I could call to fix it all, or at least reassure me that I can fix it all.

I know that things aren't alright for you a lot of the time as well. You're both so unwell, and I want to pick up the phone and ask if you're frightened, or lonely, or overwhelmed, or hurting. But

I don't. I don't even know why I don't, but we don't really have that kind of relationship, do we?

I gripe that you don't know me, but I don't know you either … I want to. I feel like I'm still that confused and angry thirteen-year-old in your mind, and no matter what I do I can't ever be anything else. These things that happened, they were things that happened (to me and by me) but they're not who I am. The seeming stranger who had no more idea how to reach me than I had to be reached, I know that's not who you are either.

I'm not writing this to blame you — relationships swing both ways, I know that — just to tell you that I wish it were different.

It feels to me like our relationship is a ripple, a diminishing echo of the relationship that you had with Grandma too. Like it's playing over again. I was pretty young when she died, but I know that you've always nursed a wound there, like you wanted to say so much to her, but didn't. It looks so familiar, but I've never asked you about it because I think it's on that secret list of below-the-surface things that we don't seem to talk about. I'm not even sure of the entirety of what's on that list because we haven't talked about that either.

I have these beautiful tactile memories from when I was very young, of snuggling next to you in your Marks & Spencer velour dressing gown with the little flowers embroidered on it, warm and soft. Of sitting in the back garden and feeling the rough concrete of those ubiquitous block partitions between semis. I remember the bellyache of eating raw cooking apples from our tree (that you'd told us not to), and the betrayal of watching your gooseberries grow and look delicious but taste vile when finally they were ripe. These memories don't really fit in with my letter, but I wanted to tell you about them anyways. Sorry for the random paragraph.

Anyways — the guesthouse that I built? That was in case you needed it if you got sicker, but I think I forgot to tell you that (or avoided telling you that because emotional stuff is difficult, whatever). We bought such a huge house this time so that there'd be room to take care of you, all the while not saying out loud, but kind of knowing, that you probably wouldn't want to be taken care of. Please let me take care of you — I'm a nurse now, it's what I do. I got good marks in Bandaids 101 and Advanced Boogerwiping. They even let me near real people.

I love you, Mum, even if it always sounds awkward when we say it.

Yolanda xoxox

8

Transverse

KAI'S COMING OUT changed nothing about how we feel about him, how we treat him or what we expect of him. He's still exactly the same taciturn, incorrigibly messy teenager that he was the day before. There was a significant change in *his* life, though. Suddenly, he was happy. He wore a beaming grin that didn't go away for days.

In fact, I must admit to feeling an overwhelming sense of relief at his announcement.

In the first instance, because of all the things that he could have been preparing to declare, being transgender and wishing to acknowledge his preferred gender expression is definitely towards the harmless end of the list. He could have been confessing a truly egregious secret – that he'd joined a bizarre death cult (like the Church of England or something) or that he'd voted LNP. Some things aren't so easily forgiven. In the light of the possibilities that run through a parent's head at times like these, I can imagine *so* much worse.

On the more serious side, because finally here was an explanation. The turmoil of the last few years; his depression, social withdrawal, and difficulties at school and with our relationships. We'd all felt so utterly helpless, watching his life career out of control and being at a loss to know what to do. Finally, here was something I could fix ... no, not fix. He's not broken. I mean more that here was something I could make right. Kai could be happy again, and it was so easily within my reach.

People keep asking if I've always known deep down that there was something different about Kai, or if he manifested 'boyish' traits from an early age. But those questions presuppose a way of looking at a child through gendered goggles. It's also kinda tiresome. Please stop doing it.

Though, it's true, he's always preferred things generally associated with masculinity – I've got more pictures of him in puddles and playing with bugs than I do of him in skirts, and I only have those few because he was forced to wear school uniform dresses to attend classes (and because of that formal dress incident). But we never paid it any mind. His favourite colour has always been purple, and he's always liked kittens. Why are any of these 'boy' or 'girl' things to like?

I've long understood the word 'feminine' to mean simply:

pertaining to the female. So whatever a female is, is feminine. It is what a woman is that dictates what is feminine, not what is feminine that dictates what a woman should be. A person might conjure up mental images of dainty features, makeup, high heels and pink, frothy things as their baseline, but boots and dungarees and chainsaws work just as well as feminine accessories for me.

It never occurred to me that Kai wasn't 'girlish', because Kai was just Kai. He liked the things that he liked and didn't like those he didn't, and that's the way he was. I never expected him to be other than he was, so I was always pleased that he was as he was. If that makes any sense to you at all?

~

Now here Kai was, standing in front of me, and everything seemed to slot into place.

'Have you told Guy?' I asked.

I'd never have admitted it out loud, but it probably would have bugged me if Guy already knew. He and Kai have always had this sort of buddy relationship, an easy friendship without the parental baggage of authority and disgust at his messy bedroom that I've kinda envied for a while.

'Not yet,' Kai said.

It made my chest puff a little that I was first.

'Your study was closest,' he added.

'Oh. Okay. You should probably go tell him.'

My pridey chest balloon deflated. So much for that.

Kai went into the bedroom for a few minutes. There was some muffled talking, and then he came out. He was still smiling as he walked past my study, so I guessed Guy had been fine with it too. Not that I was expecting that he wouldn't be – it all just seemed like an anti-climax of sorts. Kai had had this huge and profound personal revelation, and a few minutes of conversation was all he got? Seemed like it should at least warrant a cake or something.

I poked my head out of the study and called down the hallway after Kai. 'Hey, do you want us to use other pronouns?'

'If you want to,' he said, in that nonchalant, carefully uncaring way that he only ever uses to agree to something that's really important to him, and he disappeared back into his room.

'Okay.'

I went back to playing *World of Warcraft*. Yeah, I know, I so want to be able to write that I was engaging in practical and productive pursuits when he interrupted me. Doing growed-up stuff, like my taxes or pestering my local member about potholes. But I'm aiming for authenticity here, so I should probably be honest.

I did spend time that afternoon pondering the many different, better ways that I could have reacted. You know how sometimes after an important confrontation or revelation, you replay it over and over in your head to try and figure out what you should have said? It could have been so much more awesome if I'd had time to plan.

There's a scene at the very end of the movie *Some Like It Hot*, after the passionate curtain-closing kiss with the leading lady (Monroe) in the back of the boat, where Joe (who has been masquerading as a woman) is trying to convince Osgood (who loves Joe) that they can't get married. Joe tells Osgood that he smokes, that he can't have children, that he's not a natural blonde – anything he can think of. Osgood just doesn't care, because he loves him. When Joe finally throws his wig off in frustration and says, 'Osgood, I'm a man', Osgood doesn't blink. He keeps merrily driving the boat and says, 'Well, nobody's perfect.'

If I could have a do-over, that's what I'd say. Then we'd fall into a hysterical punny movie-off:

'Of all the families in all the world, you had to walk into mine.'

'You had me at homo.'

'Oh good. For a moment there, I thought we were in trouble.'

'Balls? Where we're going, we don't need balls.' Or quite possibly, 'Balls? We don't need no stinking balls!'

Then we'd laugh and hug, and just get on with things.

Mikey took it pretty much the same way as the rest of us. I wasn't privy to their conversation either. Our house is a long shape, open plan with a big U-shaped kitchen and all the common rooms in the middle. It has two ends: the sprogs in one end, and the master suite and study in the other. It's as though the house was built for a family with reclusive teenagers, but it does tend to make me feel disconnected from them – venturing to the 'other side' to listen in on their conversations would take expedition planning. But I know they've maintained the paradoxical sibling hatred underpinned by fierce protective loyalty that they've always had, so I feel safe making assumptions there too. And to save my own face, it's likely that Mikey was interrupted playing *Minecraft* or *Terraria* as well. So ner.

~

We all settled down into it fairly well. Kai seemed at once relieved and excited to finally be acknowledging something that had eaten away at him for so long, since before he even had words for it. For the rest of us, I think we just enjoyed the peace of it. When one person in the family is so unhappy, the rest feel it. It was nice to shoo that grey cloud away.

I didn't need to take him clothes shopping or to get his hair cut or anything – he'd been dressing in gender-neutral ways and wearing his hair short for years. I wasn't being entirely trite when I said that not much changed except the pronouns: that's how it was. Though, I think a clothes-shopping expedition should, when possible and wanted, become part of the coming-out ritual for sprogs like Kai. It can be really hard to look male and walk into a women's clothing shop alone to buy things for yourself, and vice versa. Plenty of young transgender kids don't have the financial resources to dress the way they'd like to without parental approval. Having somebody you love come too can make all the difference.

Can someone out there smarter than me please spend their marketing diversity inclusion budget on figuring out a way to make sproggets feel more comfortable when they buy clothes? That'd be great. (Also, when you do this, bloody well consult the transgender community: don't leave it up to Frank in PR to take care of this in between his racquetball game and his dentist appointment.)

Telling other people was interesting. When it came to people in Kai's day-to-day, we didn't make an active decision to 'go forth and spread the news!' or anything, but they were told as needed, when it came up. Mostly the response was positive, and people slipped into saying 'he' and 'him'. I heard a couple of irksome 'oh well, of course, I always knew!' from those determined to out-progressive everybody else. How could you have known? *He* didn't even know.

Kai made an announcement on Facebook, something along the lines of 'by the way, I'm a dude', but more eloquent than that. All the people who matter responded positively and wished him the best, and it seemed like one more step closer to him being him.

All at once Kai seemed incredibly brave, yet even more fragile to me. For a while it felt like I was walking around behind him, dukes at the ready, in case anybody dared hurt him. I'm not sure I'll ever really get rid of that feeling. I don't mean that he seems brave to be transgender, or to imply that there's anything lesser about being transgender by saying that he is brave – but to stand in front of the world and say, 'This is me', when you already know the world to be a hostile place, *that's* courageous.

If I've struggled with any aspect of Kai coming out, it's been the little corner of my head that feels as though he's defected to the other side. I know it sounds ridiculous, and it is ridiculous, but there's a tiny voice in there that whispers to me when I'm reading stories about women through history – strong and powerful women who've shattered glass ceilings and fought tooth and nail for our equality. It feels as if Kai's eschewed this mighty legacy that he should have inherited and shirked his duty to continue on with the battle. Or something.

I told him that once, and he just laughed at me. 'Mum, I'm a man, but I'm still a feminist.'

And now, to keep ourselves amused, we make jokes about whether or not his transgender disadvantage is cancelled out by his male privilege (it's not). Such is our table talk.

Kai

Before I came out to Mum, I made sure that she wasn't killing a boss on *World of Warcraft* – anybody who's ever interrupted a gamer in the middle of a boss-kill knows that you can lose limbs for that crime, and I wasn't about to risk that. She'd accept me for being transgender, but being disowned for causing a Heroic Lich King fuck-up in the Icecrown Citadel was a very real possibility. Mikey and I have both always known that. No parent is perfect.

It was short and sweet and went about as I thought it would, but on the inside my heart was flipping out. She just hugged me and said it was fine.

It was even shorter telling Guy and Mikey. This thing that had seemed so huge in my head was cut to its actual size.

But while there was a sense of relief, there was also some dread, because now it was real and open, and now everybody would know.

I still had to tell my friends and the rest of the extended family, but not only that, I have to do a mini 'coming out' to every new person who I come into contact with. There's always the fear of how they're going to react when I correct them on the gender pronoun that I use. It took a little while to realise that with support, even this would be okay.

I decided to put up a Facebook status because I wanted to change my name and gender to reflect me coming out. I didn't spend much time thinking about privacy, and whether or not I would like to 'pass' (i.e. be considered male without people knowing that I hadn't always presented that way) later on in my life – to do that requires a somewhat more discreet transition than I've had. But I don't regret now being forever known as transgender, especially given that it has helped other people in their transition journey.

I know that Mum beats herself up about outing me to the world with her 'retraction', and I know that she would probably like to turn back time, but I'm okay with it. Even though being thrust into a public spotlight isn't the funnest thing that I can think of, so much good has come of it that I can't bring myself to regret it in the slightest.

A lot of pressure is put on trans people to 'pass', and there's a too-widely held notion that they are somehow failing if they don't entirely achieve the gender representation that they're aiming for. While my transition is an ongoing process and I have transitional goals with my body, who I am right now during that journey is just as fine as who I plan to be. Passive comments such as 'Wow, you pull off male really well, I wouldn't have noticed' and 'You are attractive for a transgender person' aren't the compliments that the people who say these things imagine them to be. They imply that transgender people are inherently unattractive and that an attractive one is such an anomaly that I should feel flattered to be considered that way. Stop saying this shit.

While I'm at it: 'Are you sure?' – Yes, I am sure. Being openly transgender and wearing all the crap that goes with it isn't something that you volunteer for on a whim. Think of all the minority headings that you live under and imagine how much easier it would be if you could decide not to be that. Wouldn't you, if you could?

I've had a well-meaning relative send me a story about other transgender people who have regretted their transition many years into the future. I'm sure that this relative thinks of this as a way of trying to show that they care, but it's really just a way to undermine what they see as a decision they wouldn't make for me. Mother was not impressed. She wanted to send that relative a story about an evangelical preacher who'd lost his faith and become the leader of a prominent atheist group – with the comment 'People change their minds about all sorts of things' – but I wouldn't let her.

Maybe I will regret transitioning one day, but that's something I will deal with if it happens. Right now, this is right for me, and I know that no matter what I choose for my life, I will have supportive loved ones. You can't live on ifs and maybes.

Not everybody has been as supportive as my immediate family, though. A little while after I came out, after the going-viral hectic shit had calmed down, I went out clubbing with friends in Brisbane. It was a great night, until I went to the bathroom and got cornered by some guys who took turns punching me in the stomach to show me that I was in the wrong place. (As if anybody would choose to belong in a stinky public men's room.)

I know that when Mum reads this story, she's going to feel even more guilty for putting that tiny ad in the paper. But, Mother – and yes, I'm writing this so you will read it and listen to it, because it's really difficult for me to say and I don't trust my voice – I do not blame you at all. In the big scary experience that came with the viral spotlight, I have never once sat down and blamed you. I never will sit down and blame you. Yes, what those guys did was horrible and disgusting, but that was their decision not yours. So please stop blaming yourself.

I do have a constant niggling fear. I don't feel safe anymore. Walking down the street I avoid groups of people, just in case. I know that all I have to do is correct the wrong person when they use female pronouns, and I could end up in the hospital or worse. I'm five foot two, and I hate having that as part of my daily life. But I still don't regret coming out. That's what people like those tools want. They want me to be afraid and feel ashamed and go back into hiding so that they don't have to feel uncomfortable about things they don't understand. Screw that. We don't live in that world anymore, guys, times are changing. It's not going to be too long before people like you feel dirty and ashamed for beating up the queer kid and not the other way around.

I'm just kinda ranting now because I get so frustrated that in 2016 we're still having a conversation on whether people are allowed to be themselves, love who they want and live their lives how they want. I'm not good with words, so forgive me for not being able to write it as poetically as my mother, but seriously. It's 2016. Why is it still so hard for people not to be arseholes and let other people do what it is they want?

9

Going Viral

I WAS TORN BETWEEN not wanting to make a big deal of his coming out – I don't think there should be anything abnormal about it – and wanting to commemorate that something special had happened. It wasn't a big deal in the way that things can be made dealier than they ought to be, but it was a big deal to *him*. He'd done something so courageous and taken a huge step towards his own fulfilment and happiness, and that sort of thing warrants at least marking, if not a parade and fanfare.

You hit eighteen and twenty-one and get a huge party just for the sake of reaching arbitrary and redundant ritualistic numbers that somehow represent coming of age, so why not a celebration to mark actual personal development too?

I wanted to borrow a normal milestone commemoration and tweak it to fit. The newspaper retraction fell in line with wanting to acknowledge that there wasn't anything wrong with Kai, he'd just been ignorantly mislabelled before we understood – before we *could* understand – that he might not be so happy about being carved up to fit into the boxes in everybody else's heads.

I've never been one to let pragmatism get in the way of a good plan. I knew there was a chance that it would get rejected as not sensible enough for that particularly growed-up and formulaic area of the classifieds, even as I was filling out the submission form. That particular paper has, in the past, printed things that haven't exactly been open-armed about embracing gender diversity issues, and it occurs to me that if the online classified submissions went past human eyes before they were published, somebody in the chain maybe held their tongue. Secret knuckle-bumps to that person.

I wrote a couple of quick drafts. The words 'Loving you is the easiest thing in the world. Tidy your room' bumped the cost up from $56 to $70-plus, and I ummed and ahhed over whether to leave them in. I was pretty broke that week, but it just didn't sound right without those lines and, oddly, this wasn't the first time I'd found myself torn between petrol and poetry.

There's no point doing something to show your kid that you love them if it doesn't show that you love them. Kai's room is always in serious need of tidying, and till that point I'd tried everything short of a billboard. The billboard is my next plan if a hundred thousand random people on the internet and a published memoir don't do it.

Parenting is so much easier when they're too young to realise that they can object to you invading their personal space and organising their belongings in systems that are graded and catalogued by something other than the sedimentary layers down to the carpet. I recently bought a GoPro, and after a little more wheedling Kai might let me make a time-lapse montage of him cleaning his room, with a Benny Hill soundtrack laid over the top. That would be all kinds of awesome.

~

We don't buy newspapers, as a general rule. There are a hundred reasons not to (yay for trees, for example), and the only reasons to speak of in the affirmative are the births, deaths and job vacancies. Then there's the notion that I'm not much interested in paying Mr Murdoch or John B. Fairfax to tell me what to think, but this was a special occasion.

I left Kai some spare change before I went to work, along with three different messages to make sure he went and bought a copy so that he would definitely see it, and then I couldn't help it and stopped to buy one myself on the way.

It was around this point that I got some heavy butterflies and worried that he would be upset. Was this one of those awkward Mum things that I do, which I think are really loving and he thinks are way embarrassing? Every kid should have parents willing to maniacally scream, '*I looooooove yoooooooou!*' and blow kisses at the school bus, right? It's a bit late now to worry about it – that cat is pretty far out of the schoolbag.

I mostly managed to forget about it through the day, until I got a message from Guy to say that Kai wasn't entirely thrilled when he first saw it. Bummer.

But when I walked in the door that afternoon, he was on the phone with a journalist and seemed chuffed that someone else obviously thought it was a sweet thing to do and not something to automatically hate because Mum did it. Crisis averted.

Apparently the paper had been getting supportive messages all day, congratulating them on being so progressive and liberal by posting it (teehee), and they were keen to do a story for the following day's edition. We gave the journalist a short interview and didn't think much else of it that day. It was just a cutesy feel-good space-filler that they'd be doing. Our small suburban two-sprog, two-dog, two-parrot, one-cat family isn't exactly newsworthy.

The one thing that worried me was that I'd been cleaning someone else's house all day (I work whatever comes – I am a renaissance woman of cleaning, nannying, dog-walking and mechanical engineering), and a photographer was arriving in twenty minutes to take pictures for the interview. *Eesh*, I thought. *Do I even have an outfit that won't make me look like I smell of toilet bleach?*

It got a bit hectic then. In between trying to find clean socks, debating whether to put the dogs away in the bedroom, where they'd bark, or leave them out to put hair all over the shiny camera equipment that probably cost more than my car, I half-noticed my email notifications dinging away merrily on my phone. Must be something going on with eBay's spam, right?

The photographer was just lovely. He didn't wrinkle his nose at my crappy instant coffee, did his best to make Kai feel at ease, and put up with us getting a bit silly to squelch our awkwardness. He somehow managed to make us look somewhat normal, and I'll always treasure the beautiful shots that he took for the nice memories they came with.

I think that, for Kai, it was the start of him feeling as though things were really going to be okay – that we were still a family of regular weirdos and we were still going to carry on. He was wearing a big smile, something I hadn't seen in too long.

It seemed as though this was a bit of fun to participate in while dinner was on the stove, and we didn't think much would come of the photos either. (Yeah, we're not really that bright.)

There was some 'family talk' around the kitchen bench: 'Is everything okay with you? I'm sorry, I just thought it'd be something for you, sprogget.'

'Yeah, I'm cool. It was just a little freaky at first.'

'Ah, well, it'll be something to show the grandsprogs.'

'I'm not giving you grandsprogs. Get over it, Mum.'

It wasn't until later that I realised there were quite a few people seeing the paper clipping online. My inbox had a bunch of messages about it, and I had a small taste of what was to come.

~

The phone started ringing at six the next morning. I glanced blearily at my iPad and saw that the notifications panel was nuts – then the rest of the world went nuts too. The internet had imploded and landed on us.

I stood in my jimmyjams and gave radio interviews over the phone at 7am. At least, I think I did. I don't usually listen to anything but ABC Classic, so I didn't recognise anybody I was talking to. They could have just been randoms who wanted a funny conference call, I guess.

Even though the retraction was in the paper, I'd still somehow had a sense that nobody much would see it. Seriously, who reads birth announcements? I figured that it would make Kai smile, and then he could clip it out as a keepsake to remind him later that he was loved. Like any other birth announcement.

But then it was on Twitter. Then it was on Twitter four thousand times. Then it snowballed all over the world, and suddenly I had a nicely dressed woman producer from Channel 9 camped out on my front doorstep trying desperately to sound sincerely sympathetic about me being overwhelmed by media folk – while doing her best to pressure us for an interview. Why is it so much harder to tell pretty people to piss off? Maybe my subconscious figures that they're probably not used to disappointment or rejection and doesn't want to be the one to familiarise them with it. Whatever the reason, well played, Channel 9.

It was surreal. Suddenly, instead of our usual comfortable toil in obscurity, we could google 'Kai Bogert' and get seventy-five pages of hits.

Some of the headlines were cringe-worthy – whoever was in charge of the original article had decided on the salacious 'I wanted to tell the world!' and 'It was a no-brainer!' as its headlines. Ick. Neither of those sound like anything that I would say, firstly because I didn't care a jot about telling the world, I just wanted to show Kai that things were cool. Secondly, 'no-brainer', arrrrgh! That word made me sound like an unthinking yokel. Even now I'm embarrassed to read those headlines, but they (of course) were the lines repeated in every headline across hundreds of news media sites in every English-speaking country. And a few non-English too – I'm pretty sure that most of the non-English headlines translated to 'brainless'. Gah! It's just so tacky and tabloid, of all the marks to make on the world. I really wish I could make those two lines go away.

As for Kai, every future employer or romantic interest will google his name and see seventy-five-plus pages of stories about him coming out in the search results – maybe before he's ready to share it with them. It's been very effectively immortalised, and there's nothing I can do now to reverse that.

My hope is that anybody worthy of him will see those search result pages as evidence that his mum loves him and not as something that causes them concern.

(On the plus side, I once put up a post in a sailing forum, joking about wanting to run away to sea, and thoughtlessly used my real name. It was poorly written and crass, and for years I was mildly embarrassed by it being the only thing that showed up when I googled myself. Now I can't find it.)

Being the unsuspecting and naive little petals that we were, our phone number was listed in the White Pages, along with our address, and we realised that the entire world had free access to us. It actually got a bit scary, especially considering some of the more vitriolic reactions from less-than-accepting people. For a while we felt quite unsafe, and I wished so very hard that I could take it back. I had inadvertently opened Kai up to the scrutiny of the world, and there was nothing I could say to make it better. I have a tremendous empathy for people who find themselves under that same scrutiny, but for doing something less-than-flattering. It's a lot easier to be forgiving now.

Kai says that he's okay with it – that if our story helps other trans kids to feel less alone, or helps other parents to understand their own sprog better and maybe facilitates acceptance for them, then he is happy. Still, if I were given the opportunity to take it back for him, even knowing the positive effect it's had for some people, I'm not sure that I wouldn't.

Have you ever said something and then immediately wished you could pull it back into your mouth and pretend that it was never said? But instead you watch it unravel like a ball of wool that's fallen out of your hands, bounced off your foot and rolled away, totally out of control. Kinda like that.

~

Meanwhile, back at the ranch ... By lunchtime that day I was afraid to answer the phone, which hadn't stopped ringing. I'd received two emails from people wanting to represent Kai as media agents, and every journalist and his dog was determined to be the first to talk with him. The sense of urgency of them all was hard work.

'If you could just promise me not to talk to anybody else until I get this up, that'd be great.'

'Why would I promise that? You know that it's not exactly a secret, yeah? That's kinda the point – the whole internet knows.'

It didn't take too long before I learned that the easiest way to play that game is to make your own rules. We decided that trying to negotiate with or placate the media was exhausting (okay, *I* decided), and that we would need a defensive plan. We told everybody that we would find the time to talk to them and give them all the interviews they wanted ... on the condition that they included some information about resources for transgender sprogs in their story/along with the interview and also made an effort to raise awareness of the issues faced by gender diverse people. It occurred to us that some good could come out of the inevitable weirdness.

Journalists tend to calm down slightly when they realise that you'll give them the story they want, and they back off relatively fast when you set a time on it and don't give them wheedling room.

'Are you sure you can't squeeze me in between that phone interview and the other guy who's climbing in your laundry window with a video camera?'

'Pretty sure, thanks. See you at your designated time of 9.03am after I'm done Skyping with the BBC dude who's hiding in my mailbox.'

My email inbox was just as hectic. At one point I sat and watched the red number on the mail icon ticking up like seconds on a clock. In between fighting off the phone and the deafening barks that let me know another reporter was at the door (poor Pebbles and Stinky, they must have thought it was an invasion), I tried to work my way through answering some of those emails. It was overwhelming, and a big chunk of my brain was preoccupied with panic, worrying about what I'd exposed my sprog to and what the long-term consequences might be for him when the world got bored with us and moved on.

The social media response to my retraction was predominantly positive. Later I spent hours flicking through thousands of touching comments and lovely messages, and sometimes I still read through them to take advantage of the warm fuzzies that they engender:

> Have seen it, like, 100 times already today but all of a sudden another look at Kai Bogert's birth announcement made me burst into tears. ~ @JessMcGuire

> If more parents were like these, the world would be a far kinder, more tolerant and loving place. Nobody would hate another just because they were 'different', or try to take another's rights away. ~ Kelly122

Congratulations on the 'birth' of your son!
At least he's potty trained. Job well done mom and dad; he's blessed to have you both as his parents ~ MJ

I am touched to the core. As a mother I know how much I love my daughter. When our children hurt, we hurt. This is such a warm, loving, real story about real people. What a beautiful family. ~ Deb

The few negative remarks have been so blatantly hateful and ignorant that they were easy to blow off. Mostly just a lot of hysterical screeching about me endangering Kai's immortal soul by enabling his perversion, plus frenzied woeful cries about the state of American society by USAnians who don't realise that there's a world beyond their borders. Good for a laugh, mostly:

What has happened to America? Gay marriage. Transgender people lobbying for 'rights'. The United States has gone down the toilet. ~ Anonymous

This is sick and disgusting. Transgender people are the sickest of all. Even gays and lesbians are more normal. What has happened to America? Transgender people are mentally disturbed and need psychiatric help not gender reassignment. ~ Anonymous

> Good lord. They need to get their daughter some help for her mental illness. ~ FreddyVon

Though, there was a smaller element of criticism about me outing Kai publicly as transgender that still bothers me today because it's very reasonable. A handful of people who were discussing this expressed that they were worried about me deadnaming Kai. 'Deadnaming' means using a transgender person's old name even though you know that they've changed it. It can be done passive-aggressively, in a disrespectful refusal to acknowledge a person's chosen name and invalidate a person's transition, or it can be done maliciously as a way to deliberately hurt the person. Or thoughtlessly, as when a well-meaning doofus mother uses it in a birth announcement.

Kai had come out publicly among our circles by himself on Facebook, so we certainly didn't think it was a secret or anything to hide. He says that he's fine with it now, but he is very young, and there may have come a day when he would have liked to go through life without his friends and colleagues knowing that he hasn't always presented as a man. Going viral has probably removed that as an option.

This is my regret. I feel like I've stolen that privacy from him through thoughtlessness.

~

Going on *The Project* was one of the highlights of that day for Kai. He loves Rove, and Mr Punkypiratepants' head practically exploded when we told him that we might get to talk to Peter Helliar.

They gave us a crash course on how semi-live interviewing is done long-distance, given that the show is shot in Sydney and we were in Brisbane. It's all done with a chair, a backdrop and an earpiece. My heart broke for Kai as I sat off set and watched him waiting. He looked so nervous and small, and I just wanted to gather him up and fight off the whole world and protect him from it all. Then he burst out laughing: Rove had been making jokes in his ear to put him at ease, and I loved the guy at that moment – you know, more than usual.

We didn't get home until nearly midnight, and by then we were knackered. We'd been inescapably caught up in the relentless, toothy maw of the international media all day, and it felt like they'd been chewing for weeks, not hours.

Six hours later, it was on to the Channel 9 studio to do the same thing for *The Today Show*. The producer gave us a choice between sending their car for us at 4am so a makeup artist could turn us beautiful or sending it at five so that we could have an hour more sleep and do our own faces. I figured it would take more than an hour of trowelling on plaster to make me look like someone other than a buggered weirdo anyways and Kai was too tired to care, so we jumped on the opportunity for Z's.

We sat nervously in the chairs on a very similar set and waited for our spot to come up, checking our noses for visible boogers and our teeth for cereal remnants, while repeating, 'Don't swear, don't swear, don't swear', as an internal mantra. I could just see another story going viral of the woman who casually said 'fuck' ten times on live breakfast TV.

Up until this, my secret superhero name had been *a member of the public*, and I'd toiled away at changing the world by obscure and anonymous means: 'A child was found in the street today and delivered to police by *a member of the public*.' Or, 'A shoplifter was foiled yesterday after *a member of the public* called security from her car.' I get in the paper for things like that occasionally. (I have no idea how I haven't managed to be the 'Loud Drunken Obnoxious Fat Lady found hanging upside-down unconscious from monkey bars at local school by traumatised kids' headline yet, but I'm kinda glad.)

On *The Today Show* before us was an absolutely gutting tale about a man whose wife and son had died in the Queensland floods, and after he'd lost his job as well, he and his other son had become homeless. I was making up my mind to take them home and give them our guestroom when he got given a big cheque for he and his son to re-establish themselves, along with an offer of new work, and we were bawling in happiness along with him when we remembered that it was a teleprompter that we were watching and not a TV, and that we were up next with runny makeup and sniffles. Who knew that a cameraman talent was being Johnny-on-the-spot with tissues and cups of comfort tea?

Disappointingly, most of the people who we interviewed with didn't include anything in the way of resources or information for transgender kids after their producers agreeing to when they asked us to appear. By the time we realised this, it was too late for us to address it. That left a bitter taste in my mouth. Of all the industries in the world, if you can't trust news media, who can you trust? Am I right?

The ride home afterwards was pretty quiet. It wasn't even 8am, and Kai and I were already zonked. Never too zonked to play with buttons in fancy cars, though. The driver did really well at pretending like he hadn't picked up a couple of toddlers in big-people suits and let us fiddle without saying anything. At that point, it felt like maybe the busyness of the last couple of days was over, and we'd be able to get back to our regularly scheduled programming.

~

But this wasn't to be just yet – waiting at home were hundreds more emails. Along with notes from a gazillion internet strangers and approaches by all the remaining international journalists, who'd be in trouble with their editors for being a day behind yesterday's news, were messages from everybody I'd ever known. Ever.

It was funny to be reading through hundreds of comments on threads online and stumble across acquaintances from bygone years claiming to be our BFFs and answering strangers' questions on our behalf. Where were they when we were moving house and had seventy boxes of books to transport?

Out of all the online comments, the highlight for me, personally, was a well-known right-wing American network calling me a 'Moonbat Mom'. I loved the sound of that even before I looked up what it meant – 'a pejorative political epithet for progressives'.

So many of us watch the American political Punch & Judy show from afar (though often not as afar as we'd like) and scratch our heads in bewilderment, but it's always confused the hell out of me that 'progressive' is cast about over there as a slur. Progressing socially to a point of mutual acceptance and personal freedoms for everybody in their own pursuit of happiness is a good thing, right? Surely not being progressive means that you're either standing still – happy with things exactly as they are – or desperately trying to paddle the boat backwards to some ridiculously idealised past. I guess words can be twisted to mean different things in different people's minds, slowly morphed by the constant barrage of propaganda. Look at the Australian scene in a similar way – our 'Liberal' party stands for the exact opposite of what liberal is supposed to mean.

I'm totally okay with wearing a Moonbat Mom badge. Hell, I don't even think a badge is enough. I want a cape. I think everybody should aspire to live the kind of life that makes them hated by that network. If they did, the world would be a much more awesome place.

Even with negativity like that, so many allies have been coming out of the woodwork lately. Our story is part of the recent phenomenon of trans visibility in the media, which has been complicated and bittersweet. On one hand, it's great to see any movement towards acceptance and education. On the other, it's going to take quite a bit more ironing out the wrinkles before trans people's stories stop being buzzwords to exploit. It often seems as though outsiders are gawking salaciously at an oddity, rather than trying to get to know something that they don't understand well.

Seeing stories of supportive families and warm fuzzy happy endings is lovely, but this doesn't represent the reality of many. There's a common narrative that includes phrases like 'I felt born into the wrong body' and follows a particular script of long suffering, then physical transition, then happiness – all with the family coming to terms with it and eventual acceptance. Which makes for a great midday special, but completely ignores the many stories that don't fit into those neat boxes. Seeing only those stories whitewashes and denies the ones that aren't so cut-and-dried or so uplifting.

Not all transgender people wish to alter their bodies. Not all transgender people have always felt transgender. Not all people identify with the word 'transgender'. Some people don't relate to any part of the gender spectrum and identify as agender. Not all people get a heart-warming hug after their coming out. For these people, I imagine that it could be quite hard to watch families giving out the acceptance and support that they crave for themselves, or having their feelings constantly misrepresented by a mainstream picture that they've had no hand in painting but that dictates all the assumptions that others make about them.

To focus only on stereotyped transition issues and tiresome questions about genitals and hormone statuses portrays trans folk as two-dimensional caricatures, rather than whole people who live full and varied lives, for whom gender is one small aspect.

Media outlets want cookies for doing transgender features, while simultaneously perpetuating many issues that transgender people face with sensationalist headlines and vulgar questions. When you're watching the news tonight, try imagining the newsreaders inserting random and irrelevant comments about the physical characteristics of the people they're talking about, and you might get some idea about how inappropriate and irrelevant these details are to the lived experiences that they're reporting.

'We cross now to our field reporter, Frank, who is in Topeka, Kansas, with a witness to the crime.'

'Thanks, George. I'm speaking with Marlene DeTrick, whose inner labia are slightly larger than her outer, I'm told. Marlene, would you mind telling us whether or not your breasts are entirely natural before you describe the shooter?'

'Umm ... what?'

'Which public bathroom do you use?'

'Dude, seriously? This guy just killed four people and set that fire over there. He was wearing a blue sweater and he ran west.'

'That's all great, but how do you and your partner have sex?'

I've managed to stave off a lot of that for Kai by discussing with producers what's not appropriate to ask before any interview, but some still sneaks through. Kai's taken to responding to questions about his genitals by reflecting the same questions back to the questioner. The best that I've heard him come out with yet is: 'But what do you do in bed?' 'Sleep, mostly.'

When I was approached to write this book and tell our story, I was concerned that it was just another company trying to cash in on a perceived trans cache, but the staff at Affirm were pretty insistent from the start that they wanted our whole story, not just the snippets that include trans stuff. It's been important to all of us that Kai's story is told as he wants it told, even though he didn't want to write it himself, and he's had control over what is said and how.

~

I don't scrapbook – though I'm a serial offender for putting things away in a box with every intention of preserving them prettily for my sprogs at some point – but I've kept printouts of some of the loveliest emails and comments for Kai to hang on to. Everybody has dark times, lonely times, and it will be really nice for him to be able to pull those out and know that he has made a difference. That his courage has already made a positive mark on real people's lives, whatever else he chooses to do with his time here.

Our favourite message by far was one from a woman who wrote to say that she was so touched by listening to Kai speak, she planned to get back in touch with her estranged trans daughter and try to rebuild their relationship – we were just stunned.

It brought an idea to the fore that there were thousands of other families in situations just like that girl's, dropped into chaos and hurt because there was so much misunderstanding around transgender issues and what was actually involved. Something that needn't be any more traumatic than realising that your kid needs braces (though that can be pretty screwed up – those things are expensive!) is destroying lives. I don't mean that being transgender destroys lives: I mean that the ill-informed and ignorant reactions to being transgender destroy lives.

Reactions expressed by some other parents I know who momentarily imagine themselves confronted with the same issue have varied from gut-wrenchingly sweet, to despair-for-humanity sad. Plenty just smile and shrug it off as the non-matter that it is to us, but others have conjured up Dickensian notions of themselves trudging through the snowy streets singing 'Boy for sale!' like Mr Bumble. This needs to stop.

This was very influential in the decision that we would use the retraction going viral to try and raise awareness and increase visibility however we could. Kai isn't a Hollywood star's kid from some far-off place who people can dismiss as not relevant to their lives – we are average suburban Aussies fighting average battles with mortgage repayments, forgetting to put the damn bins out and a bindii infestation in our lawn. We *are* Joe incarnate. Maybe others can relate to our story and see that they can survive with – even thrive with – a sprog whose gender isn't what they thought it was.

I think it will be a long while before coming out experiences are truly normalised at a societal level, and I don't think they will ever be perfect, but what family event really is? Besides, in the grand tradition of parents being awkward, saying dumb shit and embarrassing your sprog, why should this brilliant opportunity be any different?

Most importantly, there are other kids out there, just like Kai, who are living with a secret that they're ashamed of, hopelessly confused about it and internalising all that pain because they can't see any possible way forward.

We were both especially touched by the story of Leelah Alcorn, a young woman in the United States, who took her own life in late December 2014, a few short weeks after Kai's outcoming. While social media was having a big love-in for us and our acceptance, it seems that she was despairing and desperately lonely, unable to picture a future where she could ever be happy and find love, along with the acceptance from her family that she craved.

Leelah's parents have received a lot of criticism for not being able to understand what she was going through and taking some misguided and ultimately harmful steps to try and fix what they saw as a great religious sin. I find it really difficult to relate to that – if a god was out there and he was so intent on requiring that I make my sprogget miserable, I'm pretty sure that this god and I could never be friends.

I don't believe for a moment that Leelah's parents didn't love her and that they weren't trying to do what they thought was best for her, but these heartbreaking events are a manifestation of the notion that our children are merely extensions of ourselves until they reach a certain age, and not individuals entitled to their own decisions about the way that they want to spend their lives and develop their own values. It ignores simple human dignity and respect for self-determination. It's an unspeakable tragedy that can only be prevented by changing hearts and minds and showing them that trans is just another way of being. Not a sin. Not broken. Not dangerous. It just is.

We need to speak out for the sprogs with no voice. It's not okay that a story of a family loving their kid is something so odd or unusual. It should be the other way around – people should be this amazed that a parent could possibly disown their sprog over something so trivial. Kai and I and other families are going to keep sharing our stories until that is the norm.

~

The issues that Kai had faced at school were his focus. Many Australian schools don't realise just how big their role is in reinforcing gender stereotypes for the whole of our society, and that can make these schools an inherently hostile environment for someone who is gender diverse.

This involves everything from lining the class up in boys' and girls' lines, to male and female uniforms, to gendered toilets, to different activities according to your genitals – netball for girls and football for boys, anyone?

I don't think I'm much of an activist, but I can send emails like a boss. Truly, it's a calling. The plan was that we would email every school and ask them to consider their current policies that involve gender, given the adverse effect that many of them have on transgender students, in the hope that they might make things more inclusive. I set up www.sproggets.com to ask other people to help me – many folks wanted to join in but had no idea what they themselves could do.

Throughout 2015 we sent hundreds of emails to hundreds of schools, and other people across the world have approached their local schools too. I wasn't expecting to revolutionise the education system or anything – I just wanted to get educators thinking, if they weren't already.

The email that we sent out was:

> To the Principal,
>
> It is statistically probable that there exists within your school population a group of students (and staff) who identify, or who will identify under a GLBTQIA+ umbrella (gay, lesbian, bisexual, transgender, queer, intersex or asexual etc). The Human Rights Commission estimates that 11 in 100 Australians are described in this group.
>
> Unfortunately, it is also statistically likely that many of them will experience bullying, depression, suicidal ideation, as well as become victims of violence and sexual assault at some point in their lives – sproggets in this group are disproportionately represented in statistics of this sort. School can be a very difficult place for people who are not heterosexual and cisgender (who identify as the gender they were assigned at birth).
>
> A policy of inclusion and acceptance can go a long way towards reducing the confusion and angst that these young

people feel while trying to figure out just where they fit in the world – witnessing loving acceptance from teachers, mentors and authority figures and strict non-tolerance of bullying gender and sexuality diverse young people is also a huge part of developing other students' own attitudes towards people different from themselves and can have immeasurable benefit when they step out into the world.

We would like to ask you to consider your current policies today. Does your current uniform allow an option for students who do not identify with stereotypically gendered clothes? (An option for shorts instead of a skirt, for example.) Are your staff aware of the issues facing gender and sexuality diverse students and how to effectively support them? Do your staff and students have access to non-gendered bathrooms if they choose? How does your school population encourage acceptance, tolerance and understanding? Is education about diverse gender and sexuality issues (STI prevention, acknowledgements of asexuality etc) included in your educational curriculum? Is your school a safe place – physically and emotionally – for these students?

If you were reading and answered 'Yes, yes, yes!' then we think you're just great. Good work team. If you were thinking 'Umm … Not so much', then can we help? Can we provide you with information or connect you with local resources to contribute to educating your staff and developing new policy? Please let us know.

Thanks so much for taking the time to read.

Love always,

Kai and Yolanda Bogert

Kai

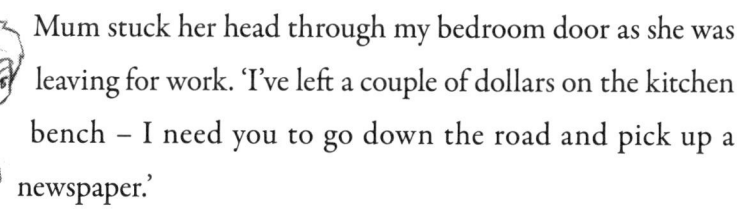

Mum stuck her head through my bedroom door as she was leaving for work. 'I've left a couple of dollars on the kitchen bench – I need you to go down the road and pick up a newspaper.'

'Okay, I'll do it later.'

'No, do it now. Seriously, you need to get that paper, there's something in it for you.'

Ah shit. What's she done now? I went and picked it up with trepidation. Knowing Mum, it could have been anything. Maybe she'd started advertising a new superhero agency. Though, it was more likely that she'd written another embarrassing letter-to-the-editor and was going to start another feud with the local anti-abortion crowd.

I read through the paper and was confused because I couldn't find anything at first. It wasn't until I saw it pop up in a post on Facebook that I flipped through to the classifieds section.

This was showing up at school to pick me up dressed as Little Bo Peep all over again. My mum has never slacked off in the dorky parental crap – it's like she sees it as a duty or something.

At first, I panicked a bit internally. Holy crap, now I couldn't take it back. Not that I wanted to, but this made it seem much more real than it had until that point. I'm not a very extroverted person and being in the paper made me cringe.

I wasn't sure how to feel about it until that afternoon when the newspaper lady called to say that they'd had such a great response to the birth notice that she wanted to do a story about it in the next day's paper. People were okay, even happy to see it – this was nice to hear, because that made it okay for me too.

The journalist asked me how I felt about it, and I don't really remember what I said. I didn't think that it was going to be such a huge thing – it was such a tiny piece! I mumbled off some things, and she seemed happy with them. Mum came home while I was on the phone, so she talked to the journalist next. Neither of us thought much of it after that, even when she said that there was a photographer booked to come around right now and take pictures so that they could publish it the next day. We thought it was just going to be one of those little feel-good stories.

The photographer was nice. He put us at ease, and I liked the pictures that he took – and I don't usually like pictures of myself, especially when I'm not happy with how they show me. I think it might be that these were the first pictures I'd seen of myself in a long while that showed me happy. It had been a long time since I'd felt that kind of happy.

The next morning, the phone started ringing really early, and Mum was pretty stressed. I know that she thought she'd exposed me to the whole world and that she was worried about it – and it was pretty scary, sure – but I don't blame her for that.

The story in the paper turned out to be surreal. It's so weird reading your story told by someone who doesn't know you, and realising what a stranger's perception of you must be.

It was overwhelming to be the focus of so much attention. Everybody was messaging me on Facebook all at once, and I was sent about six hundred friend requests by people I didn't know. Some of my favourite pages shared our ad, and there were thousands and thousands of comments. It was really hard to keep up with.

The experience was a mixture of good and bad, but mostly good. Some of the messages were from other trans kids who could relate, and others were from parents of trans kids. I loved hearing that because they'd seen our story things were going to be a little easier for them. That made me feel awesome.

Radio stations called us, and Mum and I sat on the bathroom floor with the door closed so we had somewhere quiet to answer their questions on air. We skyped with the BBC for a show they were doing on transgender kids. We even had people emailing to ask if they could be my agent. That was funny – I'd never thought I'd be somebody who needed an agent.

Journalists were knocking on the door, trying to get stories. By this time we'd realised that our address was really easy to find, so that was scary. There are some bizarre people out there. Mum sent most of them away, and I hid in my room a bit and hung out with Guy, who was just as happy to stay in the background. Some of my friends came over for support, and it was nice to feel not so freaked out. They treated me as normal. Though, it was pretty funny when Mum would update us on everything going viral. It was really weird to see my picture on hundreds of famous websites, and so many people talking about it.

Mum asked me if I wanted to go on *The Project*, and of course I said yes. We drove into Brisbane to the studio, and I just got more and more nervous as we got closer to it. The studio is pretty much how I pictured studios to be, with desks and screens and weird camera equipment everywhere.

I got sat between a backdrop and a huge camera, and I had to wait until they were ready for me. I was so nervous! I couldn't see the crew, but I could hear them talking in my earpiece, so it was hard to figure out what was going on. Carrie started talking to me, telling me what was going to happen, and then Rove yelled, 'Pineapple!' in my ear, then said, 'Oh no, I've fucked it up! We'll have to start again.' I know he was just trying to set me at ease, but it made me laugh anyway, and that did make me feel more comfortable. I got through the interview okay and I don't think I said anything stupid, so that's cool. It was really late when we got home, and it had been a sort of emotional day, scary and overwhelming and exciting and cool all at once. I didn't get much sleep.

We went on *The Today Show* the next morning, but Mum came on with me that time. They sent an awesome car to pick us up, which was good because we were so tired. The story had spread overseas by then, and people were calling and messaging at all hours, so it was nice to get away from that for a while.

I'd been planning on legally changing my first name to Kai

anyway, but after all the attention, I decided to change my last name as well, so that I can have a life with some privacy.

Eventually it all died down, and now I'm just a page on the transgender wiki. I'm cool with that.

HOW I MET MY SON

To the woman on the bus,

I don't know your name. We never really met — I only said 'hi' to you once. It was the early 90s, I must have been about fourteen, but I still remember you. I've thought of you sometimes. More so, lately.

It was Newcastle, New South Wales, and you were always sitting alone, usually towards the back of the bus. The particular time that stands out in my memory, though, there were a handful of teenage boys on the back seat too. I was sitting on the other side and slightly behind, and I saw you flinch in time with giggles from the boys. It took a little while to realise that, with typical downtown Novocastrian class, they were shooting spit balls at you.

You didn't turn to confront them, or even move. You just seemed to slowly collapse in on yourself, trying to be as small as can be. I've never seen an expression so miserable, but they couldn't see it from back there. With no reaction, they got bolder and called out names along with larger spit balls: 'Tranny!' 'Fuckin' fag!' 'Hey, shim! Shim! Did ya cut it off yet?'

I glared at them, but remained frozen by whatever weird evolutionary self-preservation mechanism it is that makes people stay shushed when they see terrible things. I wish I could say that I got up and told them to stop. I wish that I could remember shaming them loudly and protecting you. Teenage boys were pretty scary to me back then, and I wish that were even remote justification for not stopping it. Twenty years later, I wish with everything in me that I'd said something. Anything.

Something else hit you, larger this time. I don't remember what it was, just that your head snapped to the side while the bullied, frightened little kid inside me wanted to reach out across the chasm of the bus aisle and offer a hand to the defeated, wretched little girl that I could see inside you, and keep you safe. I didn't have much concept of what it was to be transgender at that point. You were just 'other' to me. But I knew what it was to be targeted — and whatever heinous sin you may have committed to become the 'other', I did know that nobody deserved that. I died a bit inside to realise that this was probably a common thing for you. I wondered how strong the compulsion would have to be, the one to drive you to be who you are, even in the face of this.

It made me think of lobsters. I read once, somewhere, a heart-wrenchingly poignant description of lobsters, and how they must shed their shells when they become too tight and the impulse becomes too great. It told a valiant tale of how, to grow, they must painfully crack their way out of their shell, leave it behind and be vulnerable to predators for a time until their new, larger shell hardens. I can never bear to see them in tanks in restaurants. What kind of monster would eat them, knowing that?

I glared impotently at those teenage boys again. I want so badly to recount a brave and fearless tale of social justice here, but that was all I did. They didn't end up splashed across social media to be righteously exposed, because it didn't exist then.

Our collective shames used to be tucked safely away on streets and nearly empty public transport — private, even in front of everyone. Hate, like fungus, thrives in dark places.

The spit balls stopped, but the taunts kept going until the boys got off the bus, one of them reaching out to tug your shirt on the way past in a cruel final jibe. He ran off, thrilled with his own douchebag bravado.

I didn't comfort you or ask to see if you were okay. The bus was just quiet again, except for the usual rattles and groans and roaring gear changes. We sat there and stewed. You, quivering a little and silently picking up your emotional bricks and stacking them back into that wall that you must have kept around yourself to survive, and me in my inadequacy — still unable to do anything of consequence to fix the brokenness that I could see in front of me. (I don't mean you. You weren't the brokenness — what you had to experience was.)

Nothing impresses a memory so deeply as shame, and I was thoroughly ashamed of myself that day. It's been a long time since then, and I've grown and changed. I've been lucky enough to share parts of my journey with some plainly awesome people, who also happen to be transgender, who have had a deep impact on my heart and life. But it was an image of you that popped into my head when Kai told me that he identifies as a man. And at the same time settled a profound conviction that he was never going to need to wear the expression that you did if I could help it.

GOING VIRAL

I hope you wear a smile now, my courageous lobster memorylady. For all the good that it does the twenty-years-younger you, I'm not quiet anymore.
Love always,
Yolanda xoxox

10

Penis shopping and practicalities

I WENT PENIS SHOPPING online with my son last night.

Yeah, that was about as weird in practice as it reads when I say it out loud. Some of the practical aspects of supporting a transgender sprogget require a bit of brain-pretzelling on my part to try and understand them, but I treat it the same way that I would if Kai had any other particular medical need. I don't see handling his gender dysphoria with love and enabling support for him as any different to anything else that I would be expected to do as a parent. I should probably note here that although Kai has been diagnosed with gender dysphoria, not every person who identifies as trans identifies with GD.

One of the most vocal detractors of transgender affirmation is Dr Paul McHugh, a former psychiatrist-in-chief at Johns Hopkins Hospital in the United States. He considers 'transgenderism' to be a 'mental disorder' that requires aggressive conversion treatment to set it right and help sufferers to conform to gender norms, and he claims that those who facilitate or support physical transition measures are 'collaborating with mental illness'. He is probably the person most often quoted or cited when you come across arguments against treating a transgender person as someone deserving of dignity who is capable of making their own decisions about their body and healthcare.

Dr McHugh has written a vast number of papers and articles on the subject, positing that a large percentage of children who present with gender dysphoria spontaneously 'grow out' of those feelings and that surgeries to physically alter adults don't improve their psychosocial situation, but in fact lead to remorse that has a significantly detrimental effect on the person. Most of the negative discussions about being transgender that aren't explicitly based on religious objections lean on these premises for the weight of sciencey authority that they are perceived as lending.

Even if Dr McHugh wasn't a strictly conservative Catholic, and even if he hadn't shown his extreme biases by lobbying for decades against every social progression from contraception to GLBTQIA+ rights to abortion choice to stem cell research. Even if he didn't rely on highly criticised studies for his information, and even if he didn't make simply awful statements about transgender people like calling trans women 'caricatures of women'. Even then, there's no reason to take his word over the lived experience of the people he is lobbying to 'treat', many of them professionals in exactly the same field, who articulate it just fine for themselves.

I can't fully understand the way that Kai feels about his body so I support him as best I can with what it seems that he needs. But even then, it's not up to me to determine the best course for him – it's for him to choose it, and me not to undermine his self-determination.

I'm very lucky to have good social support from friends, one in particular (I love you, Mr Punkypiratepants!), to ask the awkward questions of – like, 'So, dude, this "packing" thing ... What's with that?' And to smack me upside the head when I say dumb things like, 'But why do I have to be called cisgender? Isn't that just trans people trying to identify for me?' (Yeah, this is stupid – it's the cisgender equivalent of white folk claiming reverse racism when disadvantaged minorities get support.)

Some transgender men wear binders: a tight singlet top that compresses their breasts to give them a more masculine shape, which can help them to feel more comfortable about their physical presentation – but it's very important that these tops fit properly. If they're bound too tightly, there can be some negative health consequences. Some young transgender men, who perhaps don't have enough support or the financial resources, may use bandages or other wrappings to bind their breasts, and this is less than ideal for their health. So please, if you have a transgender sprogget, go and ask them if there's anything like this that they need financial support for. Even if you're still unsure about the whole thing, even though you might feel awkward and like you're not saying the right things, it's a great way to show them that you definitely care for their wellbeing.

Kai tends to avoid bringing this kind of stuff up. I think he's got some weird idea that it's a burden on our finances or that he has to shoulder it alone – the twit. So don't let them blow you off. Now that I think about it, it's probably embarrassing to talk to your mum about penises and breasts. Sometimes I wish I was a bit more tactful, but how do tactful people get things done?

If it's what they want, then the first port of call after your sprogget comes out should probably be your GP, as well as a specialist support service close to you for GLBTQIA+ youth. In Brisbane, we have Open Doors (a shout-out to this brilliant organisation – while I've got you here, if you haven't yet spent your philanthropy budget this year and you're looking for a worthy cause to donate to, please consider your local: they really go above and beyond), but resources for elsewhere in Australia are listed in the back of the book.

Your GP can give you a referral to an endocrinologist, if needed, as well as to a suitable mental health professional, while a support service can help with a million other things that haven't even occurred to you yet. It's at this point that you might need to prepare yourself to be an advocate depending on your kid's wishes and personality, of course, as some speak just fine for themselves. Kai can get a bit tongue-tied until he's comfortable, so sometimes he likes me to go with him to appointments and sometimes he's okay by himself.

There are some incredibly switched-on and aware medical professionals out there who act as transgender allies, but we have a long way to go before accepting and inclusive healthcare is the expected quality standard and not a pleasant surprise. It's awful that we're still fighting to have transgender issues recognised as a legitimate patient concern. Imagine walking in to see your doctor, and he is in complete denial about your very real medical issues and isn't the slightest bit interested in addressing them. Patients have poor health outcomes when their dignity and self-determination are being constantly undermined by the people caring for them.

Kai and I have seen both sides of that coin. Some professionals are brilliant. When I explain that, 'Yes, his name is still Elizabeth for Medicare purposes because his official name change hasn't come through yet, but he goes by Kai and identifies as male', I just want to kiss the handful who instantly adjust to: 'Sure, I'll switch it on the computer. Which appointment time would he prefer?'

It really is that easy to respect a transgender person in a medical setting. Professionals are taught tomes-worth about the patient being an equal part of the healthcare team, as well as informed consent and enabling bodily autonomy – and it's impossible for any of those things to happen if you sabotage someone because of their gender presentation.

~

Mum: Sprogget? … Sprogget?

Kai: Jesus, Mum, it's 3am. What?

Mum: There's a spider in my room. It's trapped me in the shower.

Kai: Grrrrr! Go to sleep!

Mum: It's okay. I got through the bathroom window but now I'm locked out. Can you come and let me in?

Kai: I can't. I'm sleeping.

Mum: Pleeeeeease, sprogget? I can hear cane toads out here.

Kai: Fine. Then leave me alone.

Mum: And can you bring the vacuum cleaner to get the spider?

Kai: I haven't even got pants. You get it.

Mum: Sprogg-e-e-e-et. ☹

~

At the governmental level, the fight to have transitional treatments recognised as necessary measures for those who seek them, rather than superficial elective aesthetic ones, is yet another Goliath facing us. That Medicare will not fund many transitional procedures leaves people disadvantaged, and that private health-insurance companies will cover various sham 'alternative' therapies – such as acupuncture and chiropractic – but not this genuine need is a point of contention. (Your mileage may vary.)

Facing older transgender people in Australia now is the dilemma of whether to go back into the closet as they face the need for aged-care services. While younger sprogs are fighting battles of their own, these are based on a legacy of people who've already fought tooth and nail for their very right to exist at all. Horror stories of the not-distant-enough past include being refused care outright and being subjected to electrotherapy, as well as open ridicule at the hands of the people responsible for their health. It's not surprising that many ageing transgender Australians are approaching the need to be looked after with trepidation. This is one of the many reasons why it's all the more important to include, in a meaningful way, gender and sexuality issues within medical training. There's still a glaring deficiency in current practice that's leading to so much preventable heartache.

'Gatekeeping' is a term used to describe the unnecessary hurdles put in front of trans folk by medical professionals before they will 'allow' them to proceed with the physical aspects of transitioning. It's paternalism at its worst. Things like a doctor requiring someone to live and operate for a period of time that they deem appropriate as the gender they are transitioning to before 'permitting' them access to hormone therapy, for example: a demeaning and infantilising requirement to somehow 'prove' their commitment to transition that can have profoundly negative effects on a person's life. These requirements exist outside mental health concerns and addressing psychosocial needs, but definitely contribute to them if they are present.

Many of them are a mishmash of dated care policies that just don't make sense now. For some people, there can be great personal risk in dressing as a gender that doesn't match your physical reality, pre-transition, from a social, professional and safety perspective, which is a reality such 'standards' don't take into account. It can also be problematic if a care provider is inexperienced or uneducated in trans issues, which isn't uncommon. The care they provide then becomes based on preconceived notions of what it is to be transgender, arbitrary 'criteria' to meet and a flawed or inadequate understanding of the healthcare options available – especially if the person doesn't meet the caregiver's idea of what a trans person 'should' be.

Not only are many of the 'standards' for care obsolete, but also, much of the information available about best practice for caregivers in Australia is based on overseas policies, which aren't really applicable locally and so make even less sense.

Another aspect is the legal one – in some places, a transgender person is unable to change their gender on their birth certificate and often therefore their other identification and paperwork, until they've had an irreversible 'gender affirming procedure' (i.e. genital reconstruction/hysterectomy/top surgery). Which creates needless confusion and casts undue suspicion – imagine having to explain your gender identity every time you present your driver's licence and field unwelcome questioning from people who have no business asking about your genitalia to justify your right to tick a box on a form.

It would be easy to neatly tie that loose end if everybody's transition were the same and everybody's needs resulted in exactly the same journey, but that's not the case for a non-binary descriptor like gender. There's no magical definitive point between M and F. There is no finish line to cross with somebody waiting at the end to say, 'Ta da! You've successfully transitioned!' Not everybody who identifies as transgender wishes to undergo surgery or have hormone therapy, and that doesn't invalidate their experience for a moment. For these people, this requirement can be viewed as an enforced sterilisation – people who would otherwise not require surgery to achieve self-actualisation are forced into it to 'earn' their gender presentation being officiated.

I can relate to this frustration, as a similar thing has traditionally been done to people with uteruses who seek certain reproductive health outcomes. Nobody blinks twice when a cisgender woman wants to have bigger boobs, but if a person who has boobs doesn't actually want them, suddenly their mental health needs examining. I can find five doctors in the phone book who will take cash to chop up my labia to make it more conventionally aesthetically pleasing and have it done next week, but damned if I can find one who would give someone under thirty a permanent contraceptive solution because that person has decided that they don't want children/more children.

Heads up: skip the next few paragraphs if you don't want to read a fairly graphic TMI medical story about my babymaker.

When I was twenty-eight, I was under the care of a gynaecologist to treat a prolapse, apparently a not-uncommon complaint for some of those with a uterus who've had children. I was suffering with bladder ickyness because of it, so it was making life pretty miserable. It was at once comforting and horrifying to discover that so many other people understood the reality of having to keep spare clothes in the boot of the car in case they sneezed too hard or got carried away chasing sproggets in the playground.

For years, my doctor had sent me for physio, tried medications and every other option he could think of before he'd consider surgery to repair my prolapse. It wasn't until a urologist that he sent me to – five hours away from home – told him that surgery was definitely indicated, that he finally relented.

As he explained that he was reluctant to operate because I was so young and it would likely prolapse again anyways, I broached the subject of a hysterectomy with him. Can't have a uterine prolapse if you don't have a uterus, right? 'Oh no, we wouldn't consider that for you. You might meet a man one day who wants children.'

Um. So I should put up with a chronically debilitating medical condition on the off-chance that some hypothetical dude that I might meet one day might want to stash something in there? If you want to imagine my head falling to my desk with a thud here, feel free.

Okay, it's safe to look again now. The icky stuff is over.
Periods. Ha! Just kidding.
Okay, where was I?

When it comes to advocating for your sprogget, you're probably going to need a lot of patience. There's an imbalance of power between patient and caregiver, especially under a gatekeeper model, where the way the doctor personally feels about transitioning can dictate the care available to their patients. It can be frustrating to have to jump through mental health hoops to appease a relative stranger's discomfort rather than to suit a legitimate therapeutic need.

This really messes with trust in the doctor–patient relationship too, as the client is anxious that they meet criteria to pass the 'gate' and achieve the outcome they're seeking, while the doctor is suspicious of the client being untruthful to meet that criteria – and so the gate becomes harder to reach. It's a brutal merry-go-round. Again, in contrast, imagine having to prove that your own medical condition is sincere to 'earn' treatment for it.

The parallel of people with uteruses seeking permanent reproductive solutions is doubly applicable in that way. Every doctor who I've spoken with just shrugs and says, 'Well sure, they're all terrified that the woman is going to change her mind and sue them', with the intimation being that women are just known as being flaky that way. And I'm sure there are some people with uteruses who would regret it, twenty years later, just as I'm sure there are others who would live richer, more empowered lives having made that decision for themselves. Both of those things happening is okay.

Everybody's journey is full of paradigm-altering, life-changing decisions all the time. To marry young, or not to marry at all. To choose this university course, or that one: there's no criteria on the application that says you must prove you'll be satisfied with this career forever and ever before we will let you study. That some people might make a different choice in retrospect or regret doing something in the future isn't a sound reason to remove the right from anybody to choose that option now.

Then, when you realise that most of these same doctors support young cisgender men having unfettered access to the seemingly more benign and 'simple' vasectomy, because that's 'just making responsible reproductive choices', their reasoning falls entirely apart. People with uteruses aren't infantile twits who need protecting from the realities of an irreversible decision by a paternalist medical industry, and neither are transgender people.

Mr Punkypiratepants has recounted to me a tale of a visit to one psychiatrist who listened, smiling and nodding, to him telling of his gender experience and promised to be supportive. The psychiatrist said he would write a letter back to the referring doctor, as part of the indicated formality to justify a referral to an endocrinologist afterwards, who would then facilitate the hormone therapy that Mr Punkypiratepants had chosen. Mr P left feeling good, but when he got back to the doctor's appointment he discovered that the letter described him as disturbed by his dysphoria and in need of serious psychiatric intervention to correct the dysfunction of his life – nothing about supporting or facilitating his transition at all.

Similarly, one of the doctors who Kai visited this year told him to come back in a week's time after he'd 'had a think' (one of my favourite smiling aggressions), and only then would she give him the referral to a specialist that he was seeking. The one he saw before that confessed that he'd never had a transgender patient before and didn't know what to do. Could Kai come back tomorrow after he'd had a chance to read up? This kind of condescension makes my skin crawl, but these humiliating and frustrating scenes don't seem to be at all unusual. Pretty much every person I've spoken to about transitioning has had their own story of gatekeeping and stonewalling. (Stonewalling in the non-cooperation way, not in the equality revolutionary rioting way.)

Kai agreed to see my GP, Dr Grimes, who is passionate about compassionate patient care and is just plain lovely. I can't tell you what a difference it's made in our lives to have access to a professional who remembers our names, never mind provides thoughtful and attentive care. Please don't ever leave us!

~

I feel so conflicted writing some of this. So much of it seems as though it should be intuitive to me. Like programming the clock on a microwave – you don't need the manual because it's glaringly obvious that you press the 'Set Time' button. Likewise when your sprogget tells you that they feel a certain way, why do you need a manual to tell you that your sprogget is a person deserving of happiness and self-determination, so you should help them achieve that if that's what they want you to do – or, at the very least, don't stand in their way?

But it's not intuitive. There are all sorts of messed-up subconscious burdens that we carry without even knowing it.

Mikey has recently decided that he likes the way makeup looks on him, and he's been exploring it and experimenting with different kinds. He's seventeen and funds his interests himself with money that he earns. It really is up to nobody but him what he wears or how he wears it, and he has his own very individual and distinctive way of expressing himself.

Last week he poked his head into my bedroom to say that he was off to school, and he had his face carefully done. It wasn't outrageous or inappropriately heavy for school, just foundation and a bit of eyestuff. He asked what I thought about it, and one part of my brain had to hold the cautious part of my brain – the part whose instinct it is to conform in order to avoid conflict – in a chokehold, to stop it from blurting out my worries that he would be bullied, picked on or otherwise hurt and to impose that emotional baggage on him.

Granted, the avoid-conflicty part of my brain isn't very strong, as you probably figured out way earlier in this book, but it was still with some difficulty that I restrained myself from saying that stuff and crushing the tentatively hopeful expression on my sprog's face when he was obviously seeking my support. Screw that. 'Looks great, darlin'. Don't forget to blend by your nostrils. Have fun at school.'

I was a little anxious through the day, crossing my fingers and toes that he wouldn't come home upset – all totally unnecessarily, as it turned out. Mikey walked in the door with a big smile on his face and told me that people had said only supportive things. Phew!

I don't say this often, but: *Yay, people!*

Dear Mr Punkypiratepants,

We first met when I knew you as Miss Punkypiratepants, and things have changed since then. We've both gone through changes — I just don't have a funky beard to show for mine.

I don't think I've said a proper 'thank you' to you yet: for letting me pick your brain. For suffering through my tactless questions and my unwittingly hurtful and tiresome comments. For being patient enough to give me time to understand what you were going through, and for spending so much time telling me how I can support you and Kai. For the walking teaching tool that you shouldn't have to be, you're a good sort. (I'm just buttering you up here because I have a few more questions, k?)

Last December, when Kai mentioned in an interview that knowing you helped him put a name to what he was feeling, there were some mean comments that he was being a copycat to something that I shouldn't have exposed him to. But fuck that. Of all the people in all the world for him to emulate, I couldn't be prouder for him to aspire to be half as compassionate, half as kind, half as freakin' awesome as you.

I feel privileged to be allowed to spectate on some of your most intimate moments, and that you have shared with me this blossoming as you carve yourself into the man you are. I want to write something that's as touching as that, but all I can think of are silly butterfly metaphors, so make up something nice and pretend that I said it.

When Kai came out and one half of my brain was grinding

gears of worry, knowing trans suicide statistics and some of the challenges you've faced to realise your growth, the other half was taking a deep breath and reminding me that there wasn't just a light, there was a big fucking beautiful glittery rainbow at the end of the tunnel, and Kai wasn't just going to be okay – this was a path to him being ecstatically happy too.

Thanks for reminding me that I don't want to eat piggies, I want to kiss them till they squeal.

Your ever-loving friend,

L. xoxox

On we plod

OVER THE COURSE of this year, in between writing this book and other things, Guy and I have split romantically. Maybe not quite as amicably as either of us would like, but peacefully enough, and his relationship with Kai and Mikey remains strong.

Writing has been therapeutic, though. It's been a great comfort to remember all our years together and our beautiful little family. That even though we've grown apart and have different visions for our futures, we've had something pretty damn special together. Now we're happy for each other as we pursue the next bit. Things don't have to last forever to be good.

How feckin' mature did *that* sound?! I'm so proud of myself.

No, really. I'm sad that the future we had planned isn't going to happen, and it's hard to lose the easy companionship and affection that only someone who's known you your entire adult life can give, but this is the right thing for the sprogs and me.

I want to make clear that our break has nothing to do with Kai coming out – it didn't put extra strain on our relationship or cause strife. We managed to do that all on our own just fine.

It's been a difficult year. I can't even tell you how long it took me to face the idea that I will be okay by myself. That being alone is not the same thing as being lonely. That being loved is not the same thing as not being alone. We're resilient, and the three of us have been hunting dragons for many years, so finding our own path now will be a piece of kinda difficult cake.

The sprogs and I are planning what comes next, and that has its own appeal. Maybe we'll find a nice yellow boat and park it in the middle of a pond and live on that. Or maybe we'll pack a swag and sign up for Mars One? Our future has infinite possibilities and even a few possible infinities – all we have to do is figure out which ones we want.

~

Last year I applied to study nursing at uni. It had been a flimsy dream that I'd held tight and nurtured in the back of my heart for so many years, not ever expecting to do it. University has always seemed like one of those out-of-reach things that are for other people, but not for me.

I knew that my sad little resume that didn't include a high school certificate wouldn't stand much chance of being accepted. Indeed, I checked my application every day for months and no joy. So I sat the Special Tertiary Admissions Test. I scored pretty high, and two weeks later the box next to Bachelor of Nursing flipped over to read 'Application Accepted'. I'm pretty sure that I cried like a giant goober. I was going to Big Girl School!

I bought stationery that didn't go anywhere (stationary stationery – ba-doom, tish!) and a Darth Vader lunchbox. I got a bit enthusiastic and did all my pre-reading two months before the first day, then had to reread it so that it was fresh. (Re-pre-reading?) I showed up three hours early for orientation day, just in case I couldn't find it, and had to sit and take tiny bites of my apple so that it looked as though I was occupied, rather than sitting by myself like a big dork.

There was always this feeling like someone was going to tap me on the shoulder and ask what I was doing there. Any minute now they would realise that I wasn't one of the club, and I would be found out. But no, my name was on all the right lists when they called out names, and there was a spare seat waiting for me in all my designated classrooms.

In the spirit of seeing how many crappy clichés I can fit into this book: it was like coming home. Like I'd finally found my people. Like I was never going to have to explain one of my silly jokes, ever again. Okay, that last one turned out to be a dud, but the rest of it is still awesome.

Even so. Even here, in this bastion of knowledge, in this revered and holy place of learning, I'm still very aware of the way that trans people are perceived and treated. The posters on the uni walls with positive messages of inclusion, diversity and harmony aren't absorbed by some people. I've heard epithets like 'shim' and 'it' tossed around socially, and I know we still have a lot of work to do.

The curriculum is full of thoughtful considerations of self-determination and empowering patients to make their own supported health decisions, but from a cisgender and heterosexual point of view. This isn't a point of view that, as a baby nurse, I feel able to greatly influence, though I call attention to it when I'm able. The trickle-up model of information absorption by institutions is definitely more effective than the trickle-down economic model, but still frustratingly slow.

~

Having a transgender sprogget isn't all funny penis conversations and learning to shave. There's a serious side too. Nothing could change how I feel about Kai, and I would never try to persuade him away from whichever path he chooses for self-actualisation, but the realities of the challenges facing transgender people can be pretty scary and sad.

I worry that he isn't safe anymore, physically or emotionally. I worry that he'll be hurt just walking down the street, attacked because he looks different, or that the ugly people who sometimes populate this world will try to tarnish his happiness with taunts and threats.

The unemployment rates among transgender people are miles higher than those among the general population, and transgender people are overrepresented in all sorts of other terrible statistics like depression, anxiety and suicide, homelessness, bankruptcies, and as victims of physical and sexual assaults, along with having, on average, poorer professional and health outcomes.

Pussyfooting around these things doesn't do anybody any favours, but it's important to note again that it's not being transgender that causes them: it's existing in a hostile society that does.

The 'Gay Panic Defence' refers to a legal loophole available in Queensland by which a person can partially justify murdering someone by claiming that the victim made an unwanted sexual advance towards them that provoked them to react with uncontrollable violence. It's not used to argue innocence of a crime, but to bargain for a lesser conviction/sentence as a 'mitigating circumstance'.

The arguments that I've heard for maintaining this law in Australia are not compelling. Namely, that it represents contemporary community attitudes – i.e. people are so disgusted by a 'gay' person potentially hitting on them that the violence is somehow understandable. Or that this defence could be used by someone to justify killing a domestic partner who has abused them over a long period of time … even though it only seems to have been used by heterosexual cisgender men accused of killing men.

That people with diverse genders and/or sexual orientations often feel unsafe is unsurprising, given the rates of violence towards them, on top of this law that borders on legislative permission for people to react violently towards them.

These are the things that Leelah Alcorn was talking about in her suicide note – the broken that she begged us to fix. To her, this seemed an insurmountable problem.

~

So now is the part of the book for changing the rest of the world. The future of the world has infinite possibilities too. I mean, we probably can't save it from stupidly rich oligarchs and the sycophantic contribution-dependent politicians who they manipulate to ignore climate change in order to avoid a dip in their resource and manufacturing sectors' bottom lines, so earth is doomed – but hey, the rest can be as we make it.

It can be a place where everybody is accepted and included for whoever they are or choose to be. Where kindness and compassion and gentleness and intelligence are valued over shiny stuff, bravado and deliberate ignorance.

No matter what your social background, no matter what your cultural beliefs, no matter what your thoughts on transgender issues, I would hope that we can all agree that a reality in which our sproggets are suffering profound depression and anxiety, committing suicide in epidemic numbers, afflicted with homelessness and experiencing vilification, bullying and violence is not okay. We're failing transgender people on almost every level, and it's not good enough.

One sprog who feels alone and bereft enough to consider ending their life is one too many. But it's not just one, it's thousands. There are so many people just crying out for acceptance and inclusion.

Please let's join together and fix it. We need systemic, institutional and organisational changes from the ground up to the highest levels of government to make this better. If you belong to *ANY* group of people, if you have *ANY* kind of power to implement positive change of *ANY* sort, please do it.

If you belong to a school P&C, can you put forth a vote for an inclusive uniform policy? If you belong to a building committee, can you suggest gender neutral bathrooms? If you are management of *ANY* kind, can you educate your staff on service that respects your clients' (and colleagues') gender identities? If you're giving a speech, can you start it with 'welcome, guests' instead of 'ladies and gentlemen'? If you're in a group of people anywhere and you overhear transphobic language, can you speak up? If you're a teacher or lecturer, can you include diversity in your curriculum?

Even if you're just a little person, with no power or sway over anything at all – even if you have trouble persuading your postie to put your letters in the box instead of the puddle by the gate – there is still something you can do. You have a voice and a vote. If you've enjoyed our story at all, if my laying our family's private crap out for all the world to see has helped you crack even half a smile, please drop a text or a letter to your local member and ask them what they're doing to improve things for their gender diverse constituents.

If you are the parent of a transgender sprog, can you go and hug them and tell them how much you love them? Even if you don't quite grok them, just love them – openly and out loud. Tell them this so many times that they get too tired to roll their eyes anymore and they just collapse under the weight of your squishiest cuddles. I promise that you won't regret it. Nothing bad will ever come of this.

Glossary

Sprogget

n.

    Affectionate slang term for 'child'. As in, 'I'm going to pick up the sproggets from school.' Or 'Have the sproggets been using my fucking allen keys *again*?'

Abbrev. 'Sprog'

    Synonyms – Loinfruit, Nippers, Peoplepuppies, Spawn.

    Antonyms – Growed-ups, Bigpeople.

Sproggetise

v.

    To pointlessly destroy, damage or otherwise render useless in the course of using, taking apart or for idle curiosity's sake. Death by sprog. As in, 'The microwave has been sproggetised again, but this time he used syrup.'

Gooberhead

n.

    1. A not awesome person.

    2. Affectionate shoulder-thwap when someone does something stupid, but without the not-awesome connotation of 1. See: Dufferbrain.

    Synonyms – Dufferbrain, Douchebag.

    Antonyms – Mum.

Douchebaggery

n.

    The actions of a douchebag, in general or specifically referencing the current actions of a gooberhead.

Boonterhead

n.

    A small brain in a large body. As conjured by the mental picture of a Clydesdale falling asleep by leaning on a ten-year-old sprogget.
    Synonyms – Asshole Horse.

Toast

p.n.

    Kai's cat. Full name: 'Sir Buttered Burnt Raisin Toast, First of his name.'

Boddies

n.

    Dogs. Specifically our dogs or dogs that look like our dogs or dogs that we would totally take home if their owners weren't looking. All dogs.
    Synonyms – Doddies, Bottomwabbits.

Dufferbrain

n.

    A loving admonishment when someone displays exceptional doofishness. As in, 'It's a good job you're pretty, dufferbrain.' See: Amy.

Gaffer

n.

    Boss-type. Not a follower. More than what you see. As in, 'We're all gaffers, Titch.'

Some general Australian umbrellatype resources

Kids Helpline
1800 55 1800 (24/7)

Lifeline
13 11 14 (24/7)

QLife (phone and online chat options)
1800 184 527 (3pm to 12am)

National
Transcend
www.transcendsupport.com.au

StarLady
www.starlady.com.au
star@starlady.com.au

Ausgender
www.ausgender.com.au

Genderqueer Australia
www.genderqueer.org.au
(03) 8640 9796

Relationships Australia
www.relationships.org.au
1300 364 277

FTM Australia
www.ftmaustralia.org
mail@ftmaustralia.org

OII Australia (Organisation Intersex International)
oii.org.au
PO Box 46, Newtown, NSW 2042
0405 615 942

PFLAG Australia (Parents, Families and Friends of Lesbians and Gays)
www.pflagaustralia.org.au
PO Box 3751, Marsfield NSW 2122

Queensland
Open Doors Youth Service
5 Green Square Close
Fortitude Valley, Qld 4006
www.opendoors.net.au

Australian Transgender Support Association Queensland
www.atsaq.com
PO Box 212
New Farm, Qld 4005

Wendybird
www.wendybird.com.au
wendybirdcommunity@gmail.com

PFLAG Brisbane
www.pflagbrisbane.org.au
30 Helen St, Newstead, Qld 4006
president@pflagbrisbane.org.au
Shelley Argent, 0409 363 335

New South Wales
www.gendercentre.org.au
The Gender Centre
41–43 Parramatta Road, Annandale, NSW 2038
PO Box 266, Petersham, NSW 2049
(02) 9519 7599

Twenty10
Level 1, 45 Chippen Street, Chippendale, NSW 2008
(02) 8594 9555 or 1800 652 010
www.twenty10.org.au

Victoria

Transgender Victoria
www.transgendervictoria.com
100 Drummond Street, Carlton, VIC 3053
(03) 9020 4642 (Voicemail)

Zoe Belle Gender Collective
www.zbgc.com.au

Rainbow Network Victoria
www.rainbownetwork.com.au

PFLAG Victoria
www.pflagvictoria.org.au
contactus@pflagvictoria.org.au
6 Claremont Street, South Yarra, VIC 3141

Ygender
www.ygender.org.au
Operating out of Drummond Street Services
100 Drummond Street, Carlton, VIC 3053

SOME GENERAL AUSTRALIAN UMBRELLA TYPE RESOURCES

South Australia
Carrousel Club of South Australia
www.carrouselclubofsouthaustralia.com.au
Venue 63 Light Square, Adelaide, SA 5000
jessicajayne44@hotmail.com

PFLAG South Australia
Contact Ralph Graham on 0414 337 568

Western Australia
PFLAG Perth
www.pflagwa.org.au
PO Box 524, Mirrabooka, WA Australia 6941
0404 594 699

The Chameleon Society of WA
www.chameleonswa.org
PO Box 536, Gosnells, WA Australia 6990

Tasmania
Working It Out
www.workingitout.org.au
39 Burnett Street, North Hobart, Tas 7000
(03) 6231 1200

PFLAG Tasmania
Contact meznew@gmail.com or 0438 692 179

Rainbow Tasmania
www.rainbowtas.org
deidre@rainbowtas.org
0412 931 974

ACT
A Gender Agenda
www.genderrights.org.au
67 Ebden Street, Ainslie, ACT 2602
(02) 6162 1924

PFLAG ACT
pflag.act@gmail.com

Police services in most states have a GLBTQIA+ Liaison Officer, who can be found by contacting your local police service line.